I0457144

ASLII
American Sign Language
Thesaurus

By Donald Cabbage, PhD

ASLII
AMERICAN SIGN LANGUAGE THESAURUS

Copyright © 2025 **Donald Cabbage, PhD**

ISBN (Paperback): 979-8-89672-244-1
ISBN (Hardback): 979-8-89672-246-5
ISBN (Ebook): 979-8-89672-245-8

All rights reserved. No part of this book may be used or reproduced by any means, graphic, electronic, or mechanical, including photocopying, recording, taping or by information storage and retrieval system without the written permission of the author except in the case of brief quotations embodied in critical articles and reviews.

Because of the dynamic nature of the Internet, any web addresses or links contained in this book may have changed since publication and may no longer be valid. The views expressed in the work are solely those of the author and do not necessarily reflect the views of the publisher, and the publisher hereby disclaims any responsibility for them.

Printed in the United States of America.

PROMINENT
BOOKS
EDGE

5830 E 2nd St, Ste 7000 #9983
Casper, WY 82609
USA

In ASL there are no Homonyms as are found in oral languages. ASL words have no sound therefore words meaning different things are not alike.

The use of a sign with a particular facial expression can charge inflection of meaning for a word. Change of facial expression can change simple open hands extended in front of the body from a simple "What" to "What????", "What!!!!!!!!!!!!", or "What's up".

This text demonstrates that a basic ASL vocabulary of 1,000 words represents several thousand words used in English. One sign in ASL represents most form of any one word in English.

For Example: "Run" is a verb and "Running" is a noun. Both words use the same sign in ASL. Represented by one sign are all forms of the word "Weak" . "Weak", "Weakly", "Weakened" are different forms of the same word in English but are represented by one sign in ASL. This principle holds true for the use of root words with suffixes. Prefixes are often a different sign of their own such as "Un-" being represented by the ASL sign "Not", and "Pre-" represented by the ASL sign "Before".

The 1,000 word vocabulary of ASL I represents many synonyms. For example the ASL sign "Which" can represent several English words such as "Which", "Whether", "Whichever", "Choice", "Doesn't matter", or "Indifferent-nce".

The learning of American Sign Language expands the student's ability for self expression. It takes language from the oral and aural mediums most common to most of us to a totally different dimension. Constructive manual or physical expression adds immeasurably to the adventure of self-expression. Enjoy the adventure.

Introduction

ASL II: American Sign Language Thesaurus

Is a companion and expansion of American Sign Language I. It is a study of English Synonyms commonly associated with basic signs of the American Sign Language (ASL). When studying ASL it is important to remember that the language is not a manual form of another language but a distinctive language of its own. ASL has characteristics and distinctive of a linguistic system. Signs express concepts in a manual linguistic form.

Compared to English, ASL express itself general in the most simple and common form of words. ASL words express concepts by manual gesture not by sound. (Be careful. It is easy to hear a spoken term in English and express it in the wrong form of ASL.)

The expression of most ASL words is in the present tense. To speak in various tenses the speaker states the tense of his conversation then speaks in the present tense.

Signs are usually expressed in singular forms. Establish plurality by stating plurality. Using the signs "Many" , "Few" , or "All" may do that.

Specific numbers may establish plurality such as in "Two boy".

ASL Thesaurus

Man	Masculine, Gentleman, Sir, Guy, Male, Dude, Human, Chap, Mankind, Manhood
Grandfather	Grandpa, Grandpapa, Gramps, Papa, Granddaddy
Boy	Young male, Skate, Young man, Lad, Male, Kid, Chap, Laddie, Youth, Sonny, Little man, Buck, Fellow, Galoot, Guy, He
Husband	Hubby, Soul mate, Spouse, Mate, Old-man, Lover, Lord Mister,

Woman	Female, Madame, Mistress, Miss, Lady, Missis, Feminine, Gentlewoman Madam, Chick, Lass,
Mother	Mom, Mommy, Mamma, Ma, Mama Matriarch Maternal,
Grandmother	Nana, Grandma, Grams, Granny, Nanny, Ma-Maw, Me-maw
Girl	Lass, Maid. Damsel, Maiden, Female, Daughter, Young woman, Gal, Lassie, Miss, Missy

Married	Wed, Wedlock, Union, Matrimony, Hitched, Joined, Conjugal
Father	Papa, Pa, Paw, Dad, Daddy, Pop, Pops, Old Man, Sire, Paternal
Son	Offspring, Stripling
Cousin (Male)	Uncle's Daughter, Cuz, Aunt's Daughter

	Dad in law
Father in Law	
	Daughter's husband
Son in Law	
	Sibling, Bro
Brother	
	Sibling, Sis
Sister	

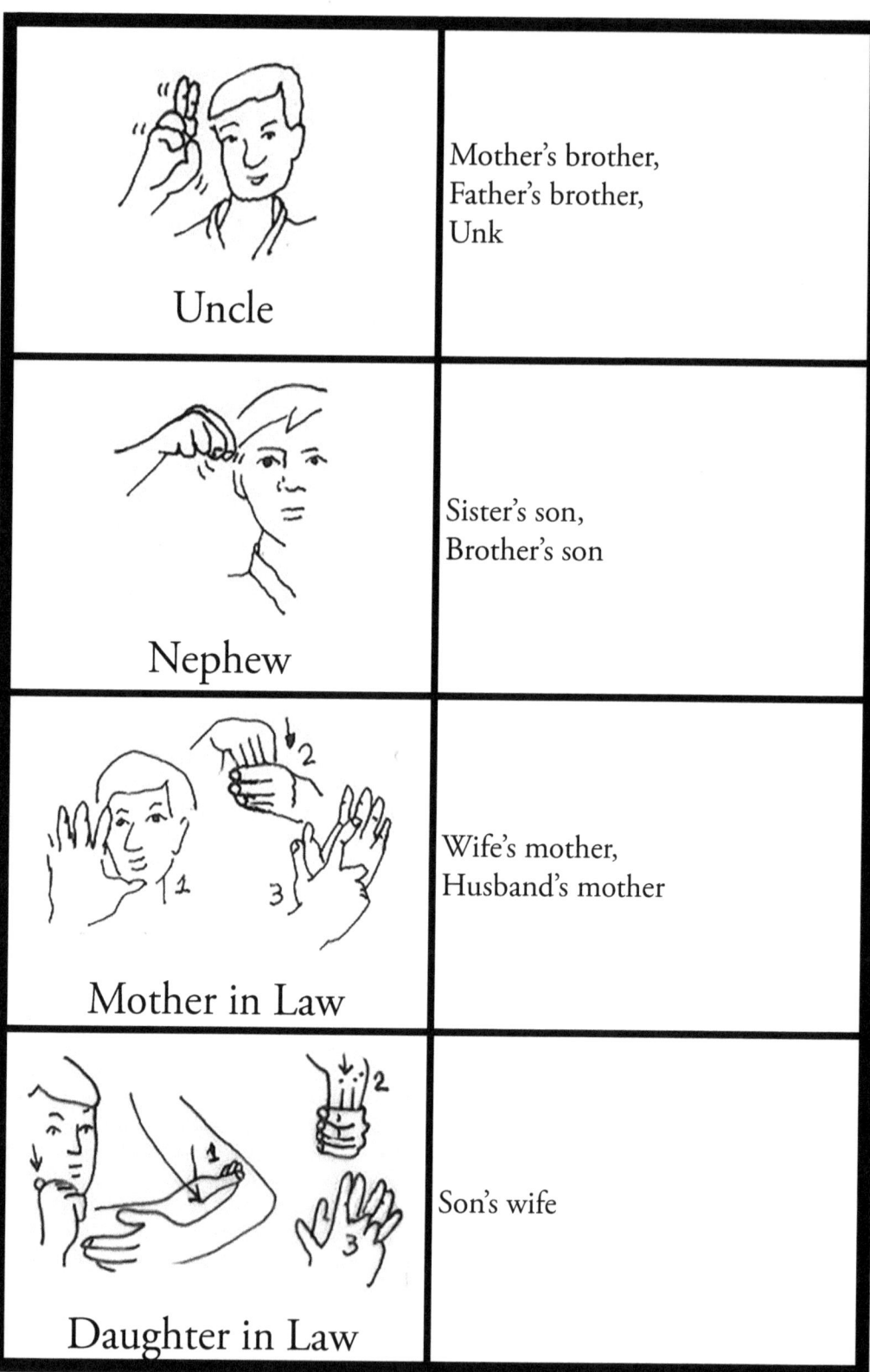

Uncle	Mother's brother, Father's brother, Unk
Nephew	Sister's son, Brother's son
Mother in Law	Wife's mother, Husband's mother
Daughter in Law	Son's wife

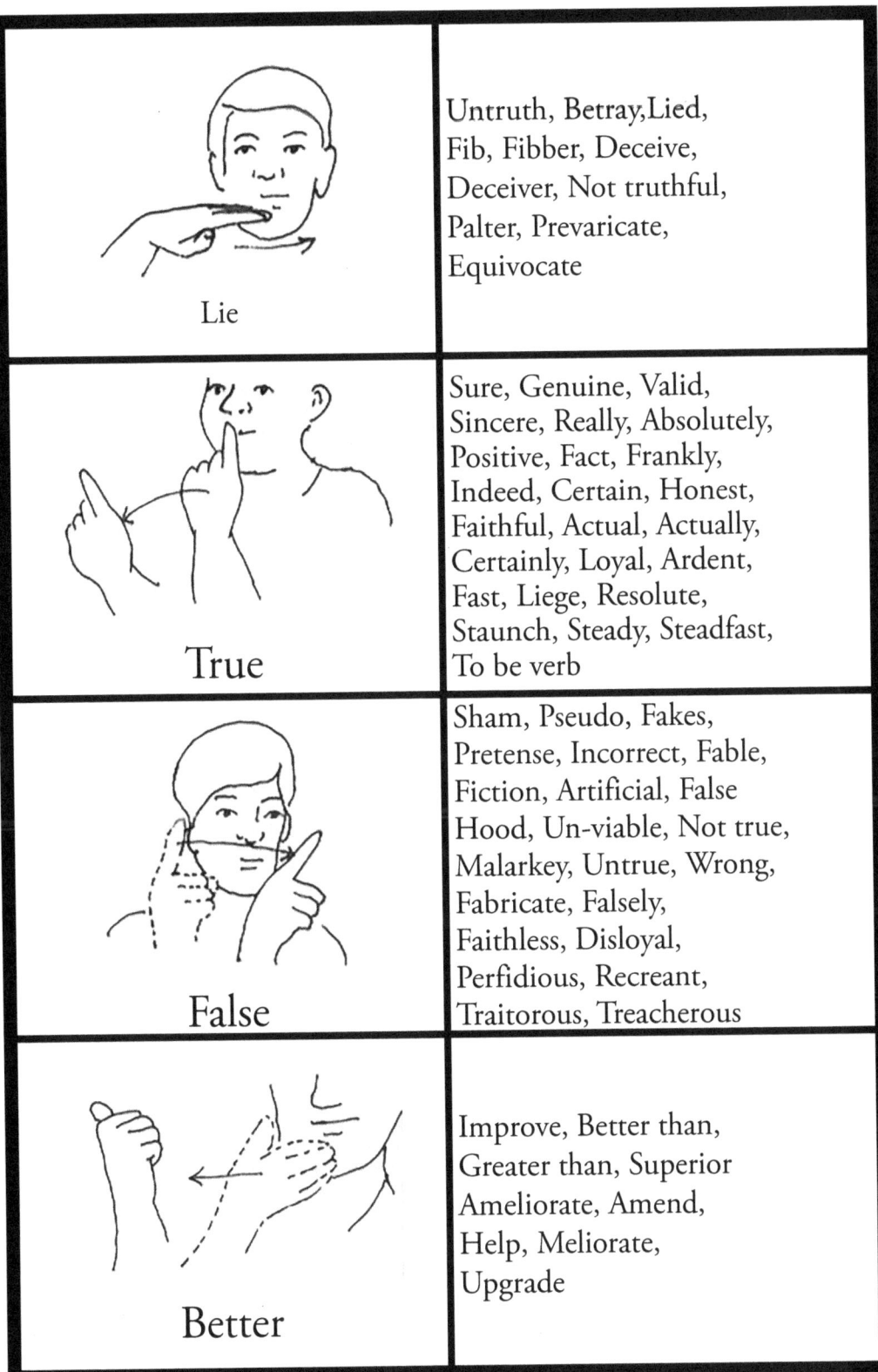

Lie	Untruth, Betray, Lied, Fib, Fibber, Deceive, Deceiver, Not truthful, Palter, Prevaricate, Equivocate
True	Sure, Genuine, Valid, Sincere, Really, Absolutely, Positive, Fact, Frankly, Indeed, Certain, Honest, Faithful, Actual, Actually, Certainly, Loyal, Ardent, Fast, Liege, Resolute, Staunch, Steady, Steadfast, To be verb
False	Sham, Pseudo, Fakes, Pretense, Incorrect, Fable, Fiction, Artificial, False Hood, Un-viable, Not true, Malarkey, Untrue, Wrong, Fabricate, Falsely, Faithless, Disloyal, Perfidious, Recreant, Traitorous, Treacherous
Better	Improve, Better than, Greater than, Superior Ameliorate, Amend, Help, Meliorate, Upgrade

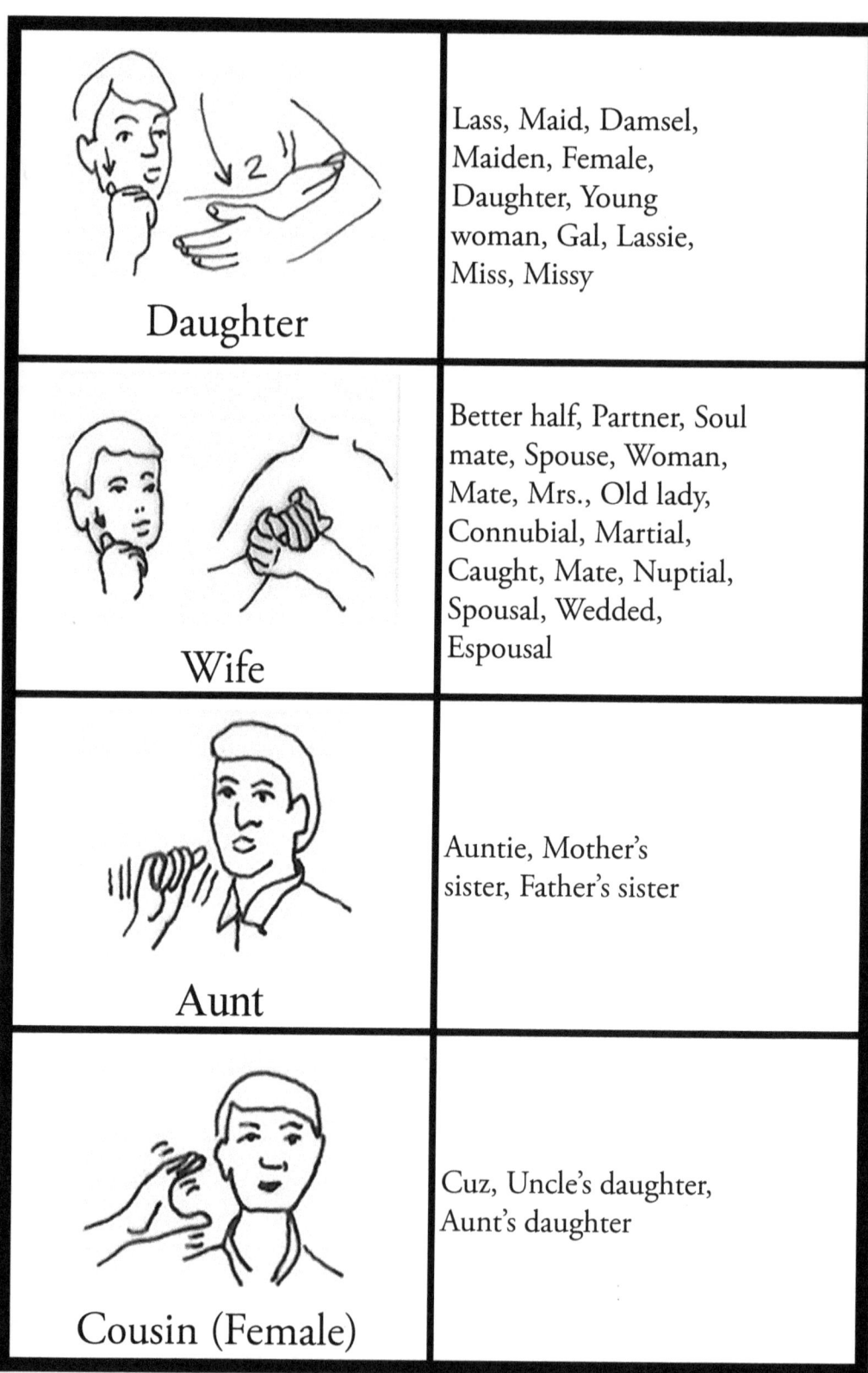

Daughter	Lass, Maid, Damsel, Maiden, Female, Daughter, Young woman, Gal, Lassie, Miss, Missy
Wife	Better half, Partner, Soul mate, Spouse, Woman, Mate, Mrs., Old lady, Connubial, Martial, Caught, Mate, Nuptial, Spousal, Wedded, Espousal
Aunt	Auntie, Mother's sister, Father's sister
Cousin (Female)	Cuz, Uncle's daughter, Aunt's daughter

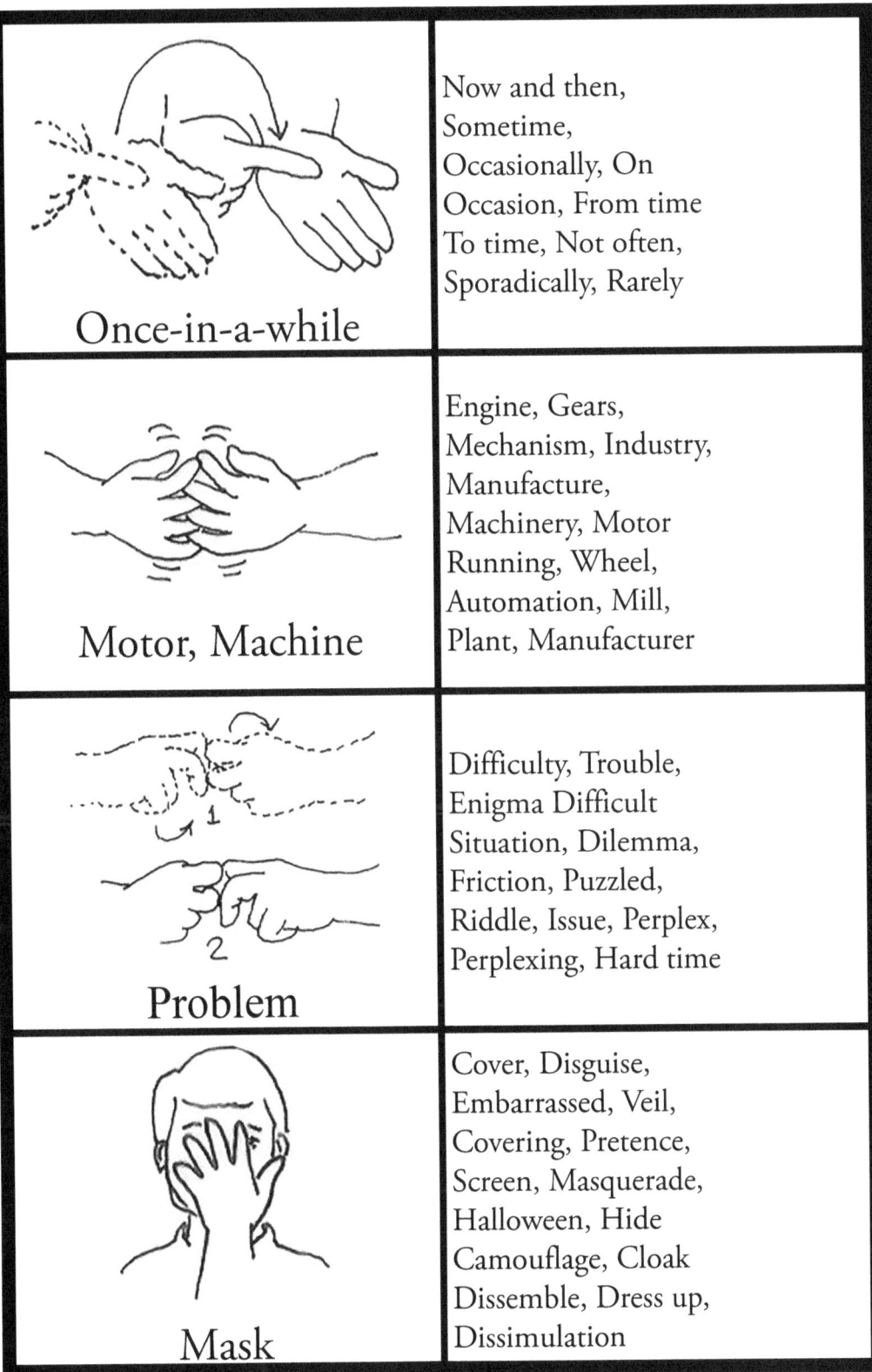

Once-in-a-while	Now and then, Sometime, Occasionally, On Occasion, From time To time, Not often, Sporadically, Rarely
Motor, Machine	Engine, Gears, Mechanism, Industry, Manufacture, Machinery, Motor Running, Wheel, Automation, Mill, Plant, Manufacturer
Problem	Difficulty, Trouble, Enigma Difficult Situation, Dilemma, Friction, Puzzled, Riddle, Issue, Perplex, Perplexing, Hard time
Mask	Cover, Disguise, Embarrassed, Veil, Covering, Pretence, Screen, Masquerade, Halloween, Hide Camouflage, Cloak Dissemble, Dress up, Dissimulation

Paint	Brush, Painting, Painted, Fix up, Whitewash, Cover, Maquillage
Future	Later on, Someday, Eventually, Hereafter, Time to come, By and By, Ahead, Aftertime, Afterward, Offing, To-be
Later	Not now, Later on, After while, Afterward, Not yet, Subsequently, In the future, Eventually, By and By
Law	Authority, Code, Legal, Provision, Scribe, Statue, Mandate, Legislate, Ordinance, Prohibition, Commandment, Structure, Rules, Assize, Principle, Canon, Decree, Discretion, Edict, Precept, Prescript

Quit	Top, Cease, Desist, Discontinue, Halt, Knock it off, Surcease
Vote	Elect, Election, Ballot, Suffrage
Gas	Gasoline, Fuel, Petrol
Against	Prejudice, Oppose, Versus

	Mandate, Law, Constitute, Rule, Regulation, Commands, Standards
Commandment	
Rule	Guidelines, Regulate, Directions, Standards, Requires, Code, Governs, Maxims, Dominates
Impress	Stress, Spire, Imprint, Show Emphasis, Inspire, Mark, Impression, -ed, -es, Affect, Influence, Move, Sway
Require	Demand, Request, Must Have, Essential, Necessitate

Think	Thought, Consider, Ponder, Reflect, Think about, Reckon, Mediation, Speculate, Wonder, Conceive, Fancy, Suppose, Surmise
Dream	Fancy, Fantasy, Vision, Daydream, Spaced out, Image, Wistful, Out in Space, Subconscious
Crazy	Insane, Mentally impaired, Loony, Loopy, Wacko, Wacky, Nuts, Nutty, Warped, Twisted, Touched, Unsound, psycho, Kooky, Witless, Disordered, Deranged, Foolish, Absurd, Harebrained, Idle headed, Lunatic, Mad, Silly, Crazed, Cuckoo, Screwy, Maniac,
For	What for?, What do you need it for?

Doubt	Unsure, Question, Unbelief, Skeptical, Uncertain, Not Believe, Misgiving, Disbelief, Confusion, Distrust, Misdoubt, Mistrust, Suspect, Cynical
Goal	Ideal, Objective, Target, Focus, Purpose, Aim, Mission, Finish line, Ambition, Achievement, Mark
Shocked	Surprised, Stunned, Agape, Stricken, Amazed, Frozen, Confounded, Dumbfounded, Loss for Words, At a loss, Flabbergasted, Aghast, Dismayed, Overwhelmed, Thunderstruck, Jolted
Believe	Belief, Conviction, Accept what being Said, Certain, Trust, To have faith in

Debt	Owe, Due, Obligate, Mortgage, Lean, Bill, Levy, Arrearage, Indebtedness, Liability
Light weight	Feather weight, Weightless, Buoyant, Easy to Lift, Un-heavy
Lipstick	Chap Stick, Lip gloss, Make-up, Lip-balm
Humble	Meek, Modest, Unpretentious, Unassuming, Lowly, Not proud, Humility

Horse	Stud, Stallion, Mare, Mustang, Colt, Pony, Fillt, Yearling
Donkey	Stuuborn, -ness, Unwilling, Persistent, -ance, Mule, Hard headed , Ass, Jackass, Burro
Stubborn	Resistant, -ness Hardheaded, Unwilling Persisted, Not flexible
Cow	Cattle, Heifer, Calf, Bovine, Bull, Steer

Idea	Clue, A thought, Inspiration, Notion, Precept, Suggestion
Imagination	Creative idea, Conceive, Fantasy, Make-up, Dream-up, Make, Believe, Think-up, Inspiration, Invention, Envision
Faith	Confidence, Trust, Reliance, Expectation, Belief
Trust	Confidence, Depend, Belief, Rely, Trustworthy

Evil, Devil	Mischievous, Wicked, Devilish, Satan, Darkness, Dark side, Satanic, Lucifer, Beelzebub, Leviathan
Jealous	Envy, Green'eyed, Covetous, Resentful, Desirous, Invidious
Oppose	Enemy, Contrary, Disagree, Against, Contrast, Enmity, Opposite
Enemy	Opposition, Competition, Opponent, Adversary, Foe, Rival

Deer	Mule deer, Hart, Doe, Fawn, Buck
Cabbage	Slaw
Cent	Change, Coins, Penny
Chicago	Windy City

Honor	Integrity, Esteem, Acknowledgement, Recognize, Look-up-to, Admire, Reverence, Elevate
Respect	Considerate, Esteem, Courtesy, Reverence, Admire, Deference, Revere, Think a lot of, Have high opinion of, Look up to, Show Consideration for
Understand	To know, Comprehend, Grasp, Discern, Acknowledge, Attain, Apprehend, Perceive, Savvy
Wise	Wisdom, Shrewd, Intelligent, Astute, Clver, Prudent, Sensible, Judicious

Hot-to-body	Sweat, Hot weather, Arid
Hot-to-taste	Steaming, Burns, -ing, ed, Sexy, Ardent, Baking, Blistering, Broiling, Burning, Fiery, Heated, Red-hot, Scalding, Scorching, Sizzling, Sultry, Sweltering, Torrid
Sick	Ill, Illness, Disease, Ailment, Sickly, -ness, Puny, Not-well, Fed-up, Bed ridden, Peaked
Ugly	Unseemly, Uncomely, Dingy, Grotesque, Defaced, Deformed, Repulsive, Unattractive, Homely, Gross, Unsightly, Hideou

Smell	Scent, Fume, Sniff, Fragrance, Aroma, Odor, Inhaled, Reek, Stench, -ed, -s
Flower	Blossom, Bloom, Bud
Bird	Beak, Robin, Chicken, Fowl, Pigeon, Fowl, Chirp
Elephant	Packaderm

Reason	Rationalize, Realize, -zation, Cause, Consider, Judgment, Mediate
Awful	Terrible, Horrible, Gross, Lousy, Disgusting, Dreadful, Yuck, Tragedy, -gic, Disastrous, Distasteful
Hat	Sun visor, Derby, Baseball cap, Sombrero, Helmet, Chappell
Summer	Hot

Wolf	Womanizer
Fox	Cunning, Sneaky, Sexy woman
Mouse	Vermin, Rodent, Mice, Weak Person
Rat	Rodent, Vermin, Bad Person

Stuck up	Snob, -bby, bbish, Arrogant, Snooty, Haughty, Proud, Posh, Sophisticated, Conceited, Cavalier, Disdainful, High&Mighty, Huffy, Lofty, Overbearing, Pour hearted, Supercilious
Fun	Humorous, Comical, Silly, Hilarious, Laughable, Entertaining, Droll, Hysterical, Clown around, Farcical, Galactic, Ludicrous, Ridiculous, Banter, Jest, Odd
Stink	Putrid, Foul, Smelly, Funk, Reek, Stench
Nosey	Busy body, Snoop, -py, Over involved, Butt-in, Interfere, Meddle, -ing, Gossip, Metal, Snoopy

Doll	Little girl, Stuffed Animal, Toy, Action figure, baby doll
Kid	Children, Offspring, Child, youngster, -guns, Juveniles, Moppets, Youth, Young ones
Napkin	Towel, Rag, Paper towel, Kleenex, Tissue, Handkerchief
Water	H2O

Bore	Uninteresting, Dry, Dull, Lack of interest, Undesirable, Palled, Tired, Wearied
Don't care	Unconcerned, Disinterested, Indifferent, Nonchalant, Apathetic, -thy, Don't mind
Lousy	Pathetic, Displeased, Terrible, Rotten, Spoiled, Un-tasteful, Unsatisfactory, Louse
Interesting	Like, Intriguing, Appealing, Attracting, Exciting, Fascinating, Captivating, Interested, Infatuating

Wet	Moist, -ture, Damp, Waterlogged, Humid, Soggy, Soaked, Dew, Drenched, Dripping, Saturate, Sodden, Sopping, Soppy, Wringing wet
Dry	Chapped, Desolate, Parched, Barren, Desert, Arid, Bone dry, Droughty, Moisture less, Un-watered, Waterless
Worth	Value, Valuable, Significant, Important, Precious, Quality, Caliber, Merit, Stature Virtue
Worthless	Valueless, No value, Not important, Feckless, Insignificant, Louse, Fustian, Good for nothing, Meaningless, Purposeless, Useless, Draffy, Dross, Inutile, No good, Unworthy, Unimportant,

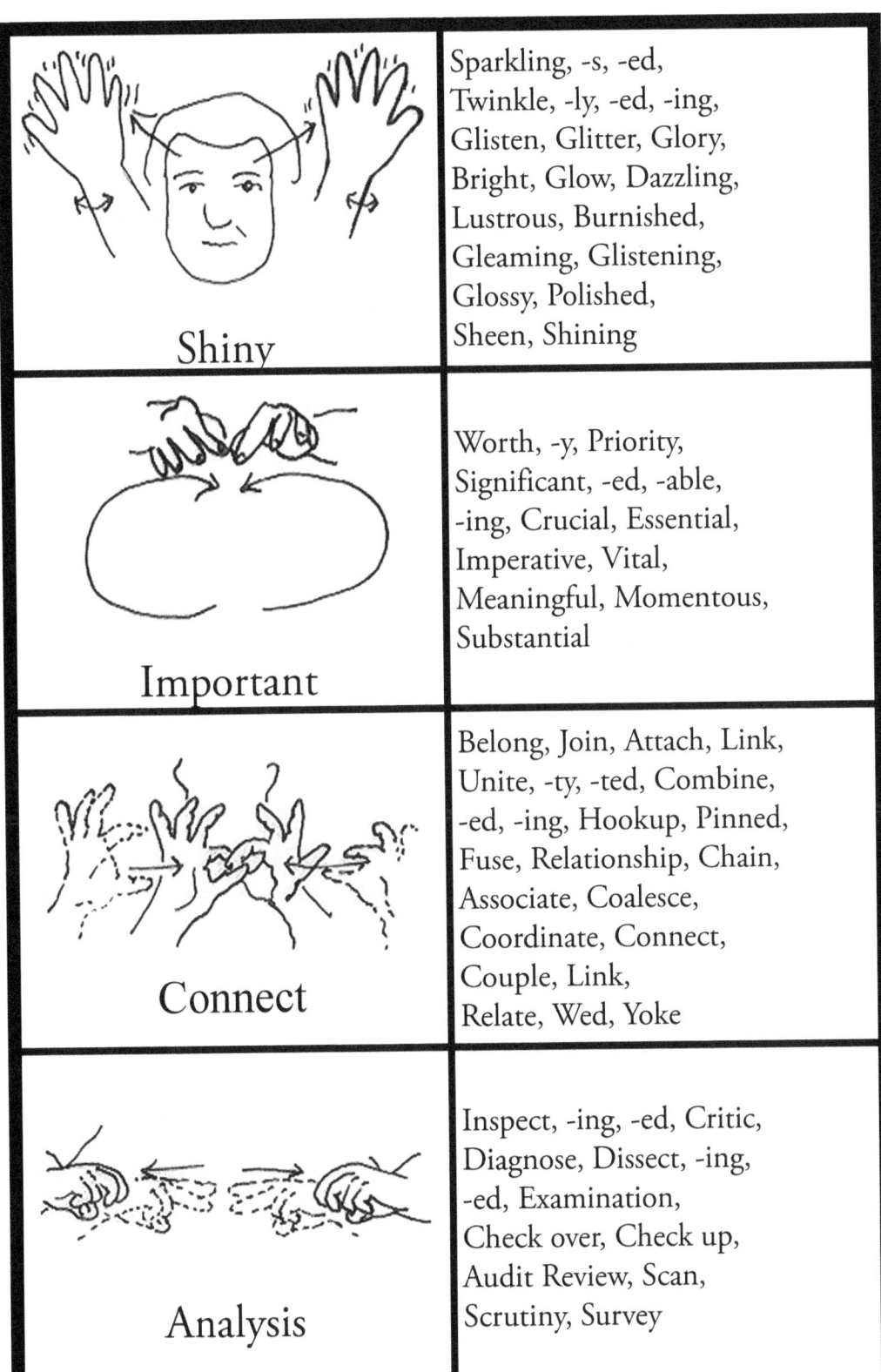

Shiny	Sparkling, -s, -ed, Twinkle, -ly, -ed, -ing, Glisten, Glitter, Glory, Bright, Glow, Dazzling, Lustrous, Burnished, Gleaming, Glistening, Glossy, Polished, Sheen, Shining
Important	Worth, -y, Priority, Significant, -ed, -able, -ing, Crucial, Essential, Imperative, Vital, Meaningful, Momentous, Substantial
Connect	Belong, Join, Attach, Link, Unite, -ty, -ted, Combine, -ed, -ing, Hookup, Pinned, Fuse, Relationship, Chain, Associate, Coalesce, Coordinate, Connect, Couple, Link, Relate, Wed, Yoke
Analysis	Inspect, -ing, -ed, Critic, Diagnose, Dissect, -ing, -ed, Examination, Check over, Check up, Audit Review, Scan, Scrutiny, Survey

Chain	Series, Necklace, Beads, Link
Story	Tale, Stories, Narrative, Parable, Fable, Sentence, Folklore, Narration, Yarn, Chronicle
Language	Sentence, Grammar, Statement, Phrase, Dialect, Idiom, Speech, Tongue, Vernacular
Any	Whatever, Whoever, Whosoever, Anybody

Interpret	Translate, Explain, Construe, Explicate, Expound, Change
Court, Judge	Judicial system, Justice, Trail, Court house, Court room, Case, Hearing, Magistrate
Explain	Describe, Description, Define, -ing, -ed, -s, Expound, Give details, Construe, Explicate, Interpret, Spell out, Justify, Rationalize, Clarify, Clear up
Famliy	Relatives, Kin, Clan, Unit, Tribe, Domestic, Folks, Household, Kindred, Lineage, Stock

See	Sight, Vision, Look, View
Blind	Blinding, -ed, -ness, Sightless, Visually Impaired, Can't see, Overlook, Visionless
Look	Behold, Stare, Glaze, Spy, Survey, Observe, Appearance, Sight, Watch, Eye, Gape, Gaze, Goggle, Ogle
Watch	Observe, Spy, Probation, Stare, Look after, Survey, Gawk, Vigil, Vigilance, Mind, Tend, Attend

Onion	Chive
Silly	Goofy, Comical, Absurd, Foolish, Ridiculous, wacky, Stupid, Nonsense, Insane Giddy, Crazy, Bird witted, Harebrained, Idle headed,, Loopy, Loony, Preposterous, Tomfoolery, Featherbrained, Flighty, Rattle brained, Witless, Senseless, Scatterbrained
Foolish	Fool, Silly, Absurd, Ridicules, Unwise, Wrong decision, Worthless, Insane, Witless, Mindless, Nitwitted, Asinine
Clown	Jokester, Trickster, Comedian, Buffoon, Jester, Bozo, Funny, Person, Zany, Cutup, Farceur, Joker

Fool	Trick, Mislead, Defraud, Deceive, Betray, Joke, Tease, Dupe, Bamboozle, Befool, Chicane, -ry, Con, Flimflam, Hoax, Hoodwink, Hornswoggle, Spoof, Prank, Antic, Caper, Shenanigan
Cold	Freezing, Chill, -ly, Frigid, Nippy, Shivery, Brisk, Winter, Frosty, Glacial, Cool, Gelid, Icy
Old	Elderly, Mature, Senior, Aged, Past, Antique, Olden, Archaic, Neanderthal, Passé, Outdated, Outmoded, Vintage, Old timely, bygone
Patience	Endure, -nce, -ing, Suffer, To put up with, To bear, To hold on, Resigned, Forbearance, Long Suffering

Seek	Search, Examine, Research, Hunt for, Look for, Pursue, Quest
Careless	Overlook, Inattentive, Reckless, Clumsy, Disheveled, Negligent Irresponsible, Feckless, Incautious, Un-careful, t, Lax, Un-thorough, Neglectful, Remiss, Slack, Slipshod, Sloppy, Ill kept, Thoughtless, Slovene, Heedless, Inadvertent, Unthinking Carelessness
Strict	Harsh, Firm, Rigid, Stern, Bold, Mean, controlling, Hard, Precise, Draconian, Ironhanded, Rigorist, Rigorous, Stringent, Un-permissive
Eye	Observe, Optic, Cornea, Ocular, Oculus, Peeper, Winker

Not	Ain't, Won't, Don't, Didn't, Doesn't, No way, Negative, Deny, Isn't
Nut	Kinds of nuts
Popsicle	Ice cream, Push up
Beer	Alcoholic beverage, Suds, Hops, Malt, Brew sky, Ale, Brew

Car	Drive, Vehicle, Automobile, Auto, Buggy, Motor-car, Charioteer, Pilot, Wheel
Which	Whether, Either, Whichever, Choice, Doesn't matter, Indifference
Keep	Careful, Care, Save, Hold, Retain, Conscientious, Conscionable, Baby, Sit, Preserve, Maintain, Cautious, Meticulous
Sweetheart	Darling, Lover, Steady, Boy/girlfriend, Intended, Spouse, Lovable, Honey, Precious, Love muffin, Cupcake, Beloved, Flame, Honey-bunch, Lady-love, Sweetie, True love, Heartthrob, Gal, Turtledove, Beau, Inamorata,

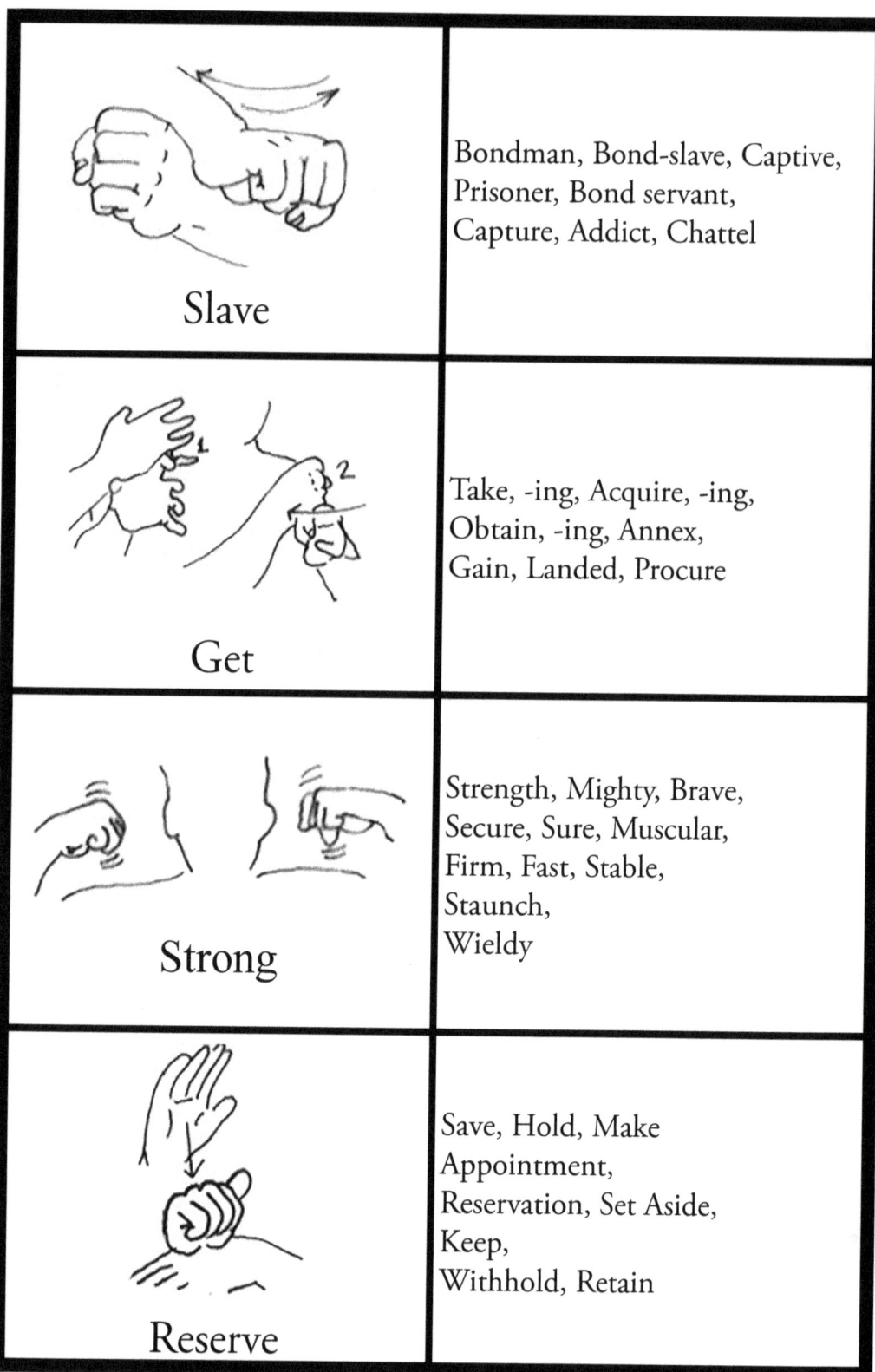

Slave	Bondman, Bond-slave, Captive, Prisoner, Bond servant, Capture, Addict, Chattel
Get	Take, -ing, Acquire, -ing, Obtain, -ing, Annex, Gain, Landed, Procure
Strong	Strength, Mighty, Brave, Secure, Sure, Muscular, Firm, Fast, Stable, Staunch, Wieldy
Reserve	Save, Hold, Make Appointment, Reservation, Set Aside, Keep, Withhold, Retain

Wrong	Mistake, Error, Corrupt, Inaccurate, Incorrect, Erroneous, -ly, Unjust, Counterfactual, Specious, Unsound, Untrue, Misguided
Say	Tell, Talk, Told, Speak, Declare, Recite, Articulate, Enunciate, Phonate, Pronounce, State, Utter, Disclose, Divulge
Letter	Note, Mail, Post card, Correspondence, Epistle, Missive
Telephone	Phone, Call up, Receiver

Follow	Pursue, Stalk, Go after, Trail, Grasp meaning, Series, Sequel, Ensue, Succeed, Supervene, Comply, Conform, Observe Disciple
Break	Destroy, Snap, Fracture, Time out, Intermission, Recess, Smash, Damaged, Tear apart, Crack, Bust
Make	Create, Prepare, Construct, Produce, Mold, Compose, Formulate, Earn, Gain, Assemble, Construct, Originate
Baptize	Baptist, Submerge, Christen, Belief, Immersion

Nothing	None, Zero, Zilch, Zip, All gone, Empty, Blank, Lacking, Non presence, Insignificance
And	Also, Plus, Include, Too
The	That, Specific
Scold	Chew out, Correct, Rail, Someone, Bawled out, Lecture, Rag, Admonish, Tongue lash, Reprimand, Discipline, Punish, Rebuke, Get after, Lash out

Chemistry	Chemical, Experiment, Lab
Science	Lab, Scientific
Pain	Hurt, Ache, Sore, Discomfort, Injury, Anguish, Wound
Bicycle	Bike, Tricycle, Cycle, Two wheeler, Velocipede

Necking	Smooching, Romance, Kissing, Make-ing out
Germany	German
Many	Abundance, A lot of, Lots, Numerous, Bunch, Multiple, Quantity, How mush, Plenty, Multitude, Populous, Sundry Voluminous
No	Not so, Refuse, Negative, Refusal, Forget it

More	Greater amount, Again
Crash	Wreck, Amash, Accident, Collision, Collide, Impact, Concussion, Jolt, Collapse, Pileup
With	Together, Accompany, Go with, Along, Escort, In the company of, Partner, By, Conjointly, Jointly, Mutually
Without	Have not, None, Absence, Lack, -ing

Save	Salvation, Rescue, Deliver, Salvage, Emancipate, Made Free, Redeem, Retrieve
Free	Freedom, Unleash, W/o cost, Salvation, Safe, Let go, Untangle, No charge, Liberate, Fancy free, Unrestrained Release, Unbind, Unchain, Unshackle, Unconfined,
Praise	Applaud, Acclaim, Worship, Ovation, Approve, Congratulate, Honor, Bless, Celebrate, Eulogize, Magnify Acknowledge, Commend,, Resound, Compliments
Pray	Ask, Request, Petition, Plead, Beg, Beseech, Implore

Use	Utilize, -zation, Consume, Exercise, Previously owned, 2nd hand
Question	Petition, Ask, Interrogate, Request, Inquire, Quiz, Imply, Remonstrance, Interrogation
God	Supreme being, Creator, Heavenly Father, Lord, Allah, Higher power, Jehovah
Never	Not, Not at all, Not ever, Nevermore

Shoe	Foot wear, Clogs, Sneakers, Tennis
Control	Administer, Conduct, Manage, Govern, Direct, Regulate, Rule, Control, -lled, -ing, Run, Discipline, Operate, Subdue, Handle, Dominate, Reign, Manage,
Fight	Battle, Conflict, Squall, Boxing, Fought, Quarrel, Hit, Punch, Rumble, Tiff, Squabble, Brawl, Altercation, Falling out, Controversy, Feud, Duel, Dispute, Run in, Knock-down-drag-out
Guard	Protect, Defend, Shield, Watch out for, Shelter, Security, Cover, Fend, Shield, Safeguard, Protection, Look out

Much	A Lot, Abundance, Great, Plenty, Large, Enormous, Great deal, Mass, Huge
Big	Large, Great, Huge, Enormous, Gigantic, gargantuan, Major, Exuberant, Sizeable, Large scale, Hefty
Small	Little, Tiny, Micro, Mini, Minuscule, Microscopic, Dinky, Lesser, Small fry, Small time, Measly Slight
Short	Brief, Moment, Fleeting, Soon, Quick, Skimpy, Snippy, Short and sweet

Want	Have to Have, Must have, Longing, Feel like, Crave, Desire, Wish
Beg	Plead, Grovel, Ask, Request, Implore, Solicit, Beseech, Appeal, Entreat, Supplicate, Grovel
Come	Approach, Invite, Appear, Move toward
Go	Went, Going, Will go, Leave, Depart, Go away, Go to, Exit, Take off, Run along

	Sprinkle, Baptize
Shower	
Grace	Unmerited favor
Methodist	Sprinkle
Light-to shine	Bright, -ten, Illuminate, Luminous, Illume, Lighten, Radiate

	Kids, Child, Youths, offspring, Brood, Rug rats, Descendants, Posterity, Juveniles, Moppets, Young ones, Youngsters
Children	
	Canyon, Ravine, Gully, Dip
Vally	
	Invite, Hire, Employ
Welcome	
	Decease, -d, Pass away, Death, Lost, Late, Died, No longer living, Gone, Inanimate demise, Muted, Extinct, Corpse, Bygone, Departed, Lifeless, Deadened, Spiritless, Unfeeling,
Dead	

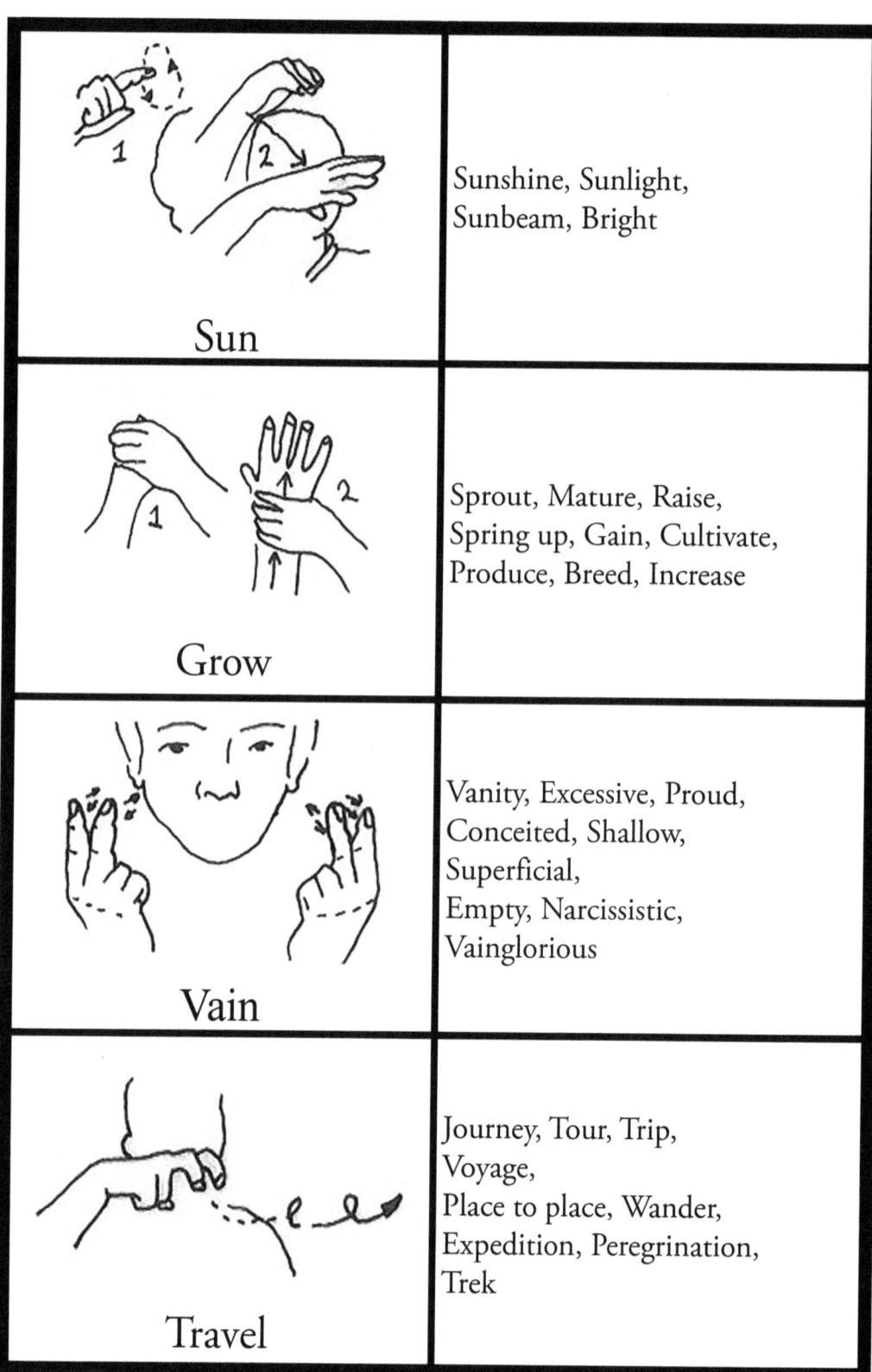

Sun	Sunshine, Sunlight, Sunbeam, Bright
Grow	Sprout, Mature, Raise, Spring up, Gain, Cultivate, Produce, Breed, Increase
Vain	Vanity, Excessive, Proud, Conceited, Shallow, Superficial, Empty, Narcissistic, Vainglorious
Travel	Journey, Tour, Trip, Voyage, Place to place, Wander, Expedition, Peregrination, Trek

Difficult	Hard, Unyielding, Rigid, Problem, Not easy, Effortful, Formidable, Strenuous, Toilsome, Puzzling
Save(money)	Savings, Set aside, Preserve, Accumulate, Nest Egg, Economize, Collect, Retain, Store, Put away
Quote	Quotation, Theme, Title, Topic, Subject, Cite, Thesis, Sarcastic statement
Selfish	Stingy, Miserly, Greedy, Self centered, Scrooge, Self Absorbed, Inconsiderate, Self interest, Egotistic, Egocentric

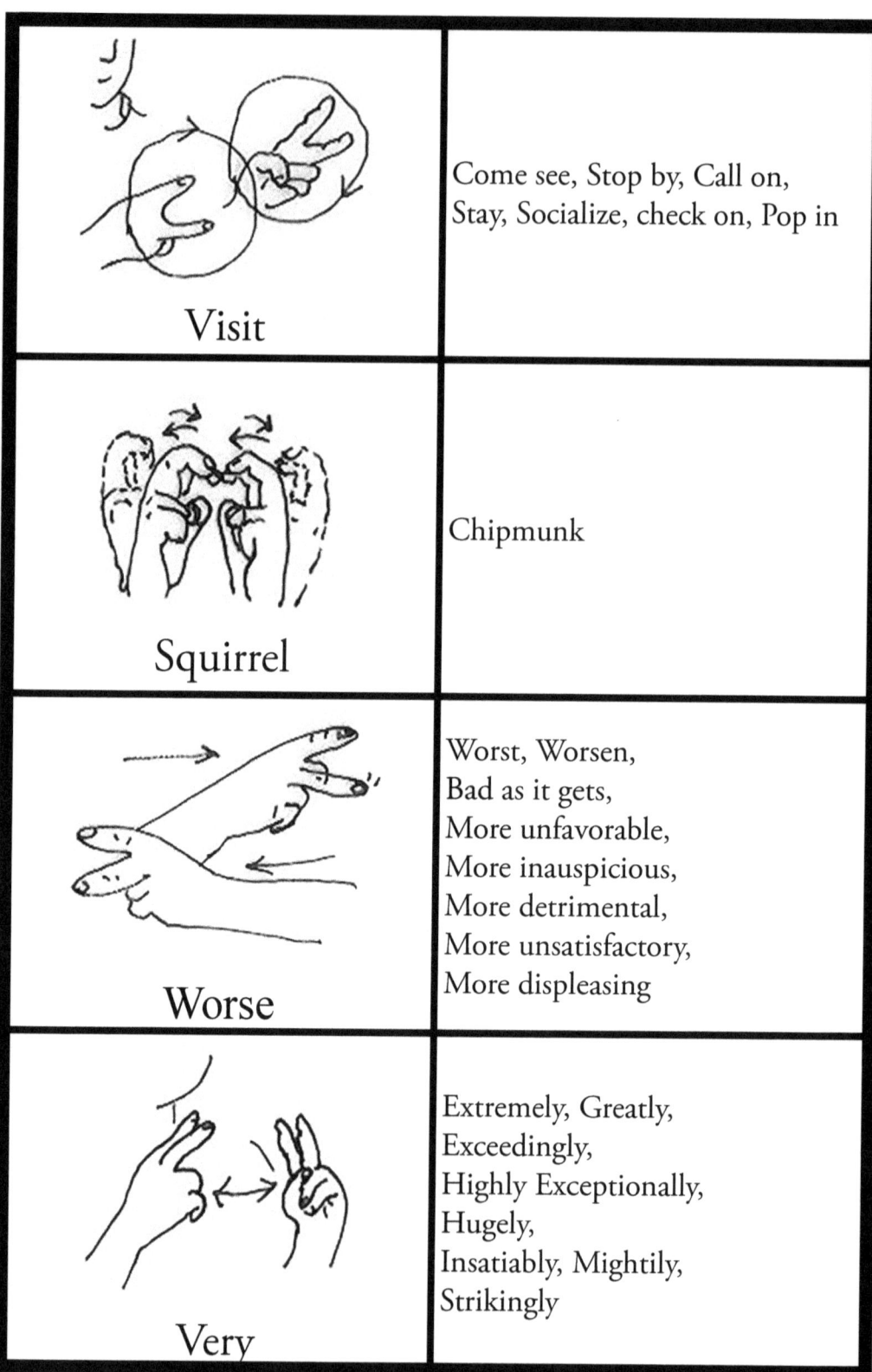

Visit	Come see, Stop by, Call on, Stay, Socialize, check on, Pop in
Squirrel	Chipmunk
Worse	Worst, Worsen, Bad as it gets, More unfavorable, More inauspicious, More detrimental, More unsatisfactory, More displeasing
Very	Extremely, Greatly, Exceedingly, Highly Exceptionally, Hugely, Insatiably, Mightily, Strikingly

Scissors	Sheers, Trim, Cut, Edge, Clip, Clippers, Snipers
Virgin	Unspoiled, Untouched, Innocent, Pure, W/o alcohol, Virginity, Chaste, Unadulterated, Untapped
Tournament	Contest, Game, Competition, Playoff, Challenge
Hard	Difficult, Not easy, Complicated, Solid, Firm, Inflexible, Rigid, Complex, Tough, Effortful, Formidable, Strenuous

Sweet	Sweetener, Pleasure, Gentle, Agreeable, Amiable, Caring, Precious, Confection, Tender, Winsome
Cute	Good looking, Adorable, Handsome, Pleasing, Dainty
Good	Well done, Well Behaved, Virtuous, Well reputable, Upstanding, Skillful, Decorous
Bad	Wicked, Harmful, Evil, Nasty, Spoiled, Not good, Unfavorable, Naughty, Inaccurate, Mischievous, Ruined, Inauspicious, Ill behaved, Misbehaving, Immoral, Iniquitous, Reprobate, Sinful, Vicious

Bachelor	Single man, Unmarried male
Kiss	Smooch, Peck, Make out, Buss, Lip, Osculate, Smack
Homosexual	Gay, Same sex relationship, Queer, homoerotic, Homophile
Disappoint	Sour, Disillusioned, Disappointment, Unsatisfied

Laugh	Giggle, Chuckle, Hysterical, Snicker, Rolling in aisles, Guffaw, Crackle, Snort, Chortle, Hee-Haw, Tee hee, Titter
Mock	Tease, Laugh at, Jeer, Ridicule, Joke with, Prod, Deceive, Torment, Beguile, Betray, Bluff, Cozen, Delude, Double Cross, Mislead, Parody, Travesty, Taunt
Farm	Ranch, Plantation, Agriculture
Farmer	Sod buster

Thank you	Give thanks, Gratitude, Grateful, Appreciative, Thankful, Delighted, Obliged
Send	Mail, Transmit, Send off, Emit, Convey, Sending, Dispatch, Forward, Remit, Route, Ship
Dirty	Pig, Filthy, Swine, Dingy, Boar, Unclean, Grimy, Pornographic, Dungy, Not clean, Murky, Stain Obscene, Mucky, Nasty, Sloppy, Foul, Grubby, Sordid, Squalid, Immoral, Unchaste, Gross, Profane, Rank, Raunchy, Smutty, Vulgar, Tarnish, Smudge,
Elevator	Lift

Jew	Jewish, Hebrew, To conserve
Drool	Envy, Long for, Desire, Lust, Salivate, Slobber, Crave, Desiderate
Bitter	Disappointed, Distasteful, Galling, Grievous, Unpalatable, Acerb, Acrid, Disillusioned, Astringent, Austere, Acerbic, Tart, Acidulous, Acidic
Blood	Plasma, Bleeding, Hemoglobin

Indian	Native American
Deaf	Can't hear, Hearing Impaired
Promise	Vow, Pact, Swear, Guarantee, Commit, Pledge, Oath, Omen, Portend, Presage
Favorite	Prefer, Preference

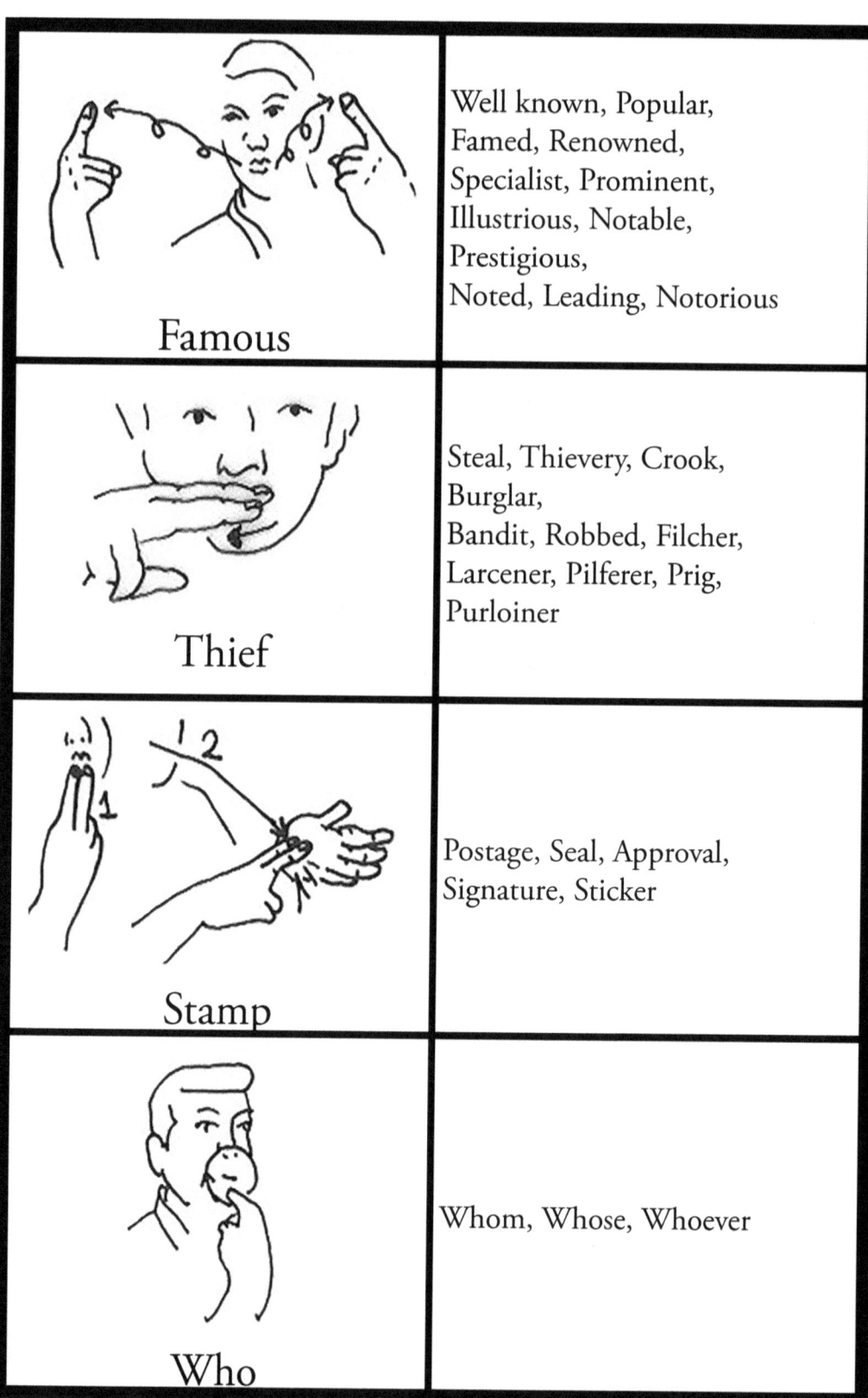

Famous

Well known, Popular, Famed, Renowned, Specialist, Prominent, Illustrious, Notable, Prestigious, Noted, Leading, Notorious

Thief

Steal, Thievery, Crook, Burglar, Bandit, Robbed, Filcher, Larcener, Pilferer, Prig, Purloiner

Stamp

Postage, Seal, Approval, Signature, Sticker

Who

Whom, Whose, Whoever

Tomato	'maters
Syrup	Honey
Sure	True, -thful, -lly, Actually, Absolutely, Valid, Genuine, Really, Right, Loyal, Correct, Positive, Am, Is, Are, Was,, Been, Being, Infallible, Inerrable, Surefire, Inerrant, Unerring, Certain, Un-failing, Inarguable, Incontestable, Incontrovertible, Indisputable, Undeniable, Confident,
Candy	Were Sweets, Cute, Sugar, Confection

Duck	Quack, Duckling, Mallard
Warm	Almost hot, Friendly, Likeable, Aglow
Eat	Food, Pig out, Ate, Consume, Devour, Ingest, Meal, Partake
Food	Eat, Meal, Consume, Edibles, Feed, Chow, Grub, Provisions, Victuals

Lip Reading	Oral, Speech reading
Hearing Aid	Listening aid
Wine	Liquor, Liquors
Taste	Kind, Prefer, -ences

	Savory, -ing, Palatable, Luscious, Appetizing, Real Good, Yummy, tasty, Scrumptious, Delightful
Delicious	
	Daily, Always, Common, Customary
Everyday	
	Chewing, Pipe, Wad, Snuff
Tobacco	
	Tooth Doctor, Gum, Doctor, Orthodontist
Dentist	

Orange (fruit)	Orange Juice, Orange Drink
Home	Abode, House, residence, Domicile, Habitat, Apartment, Shelter, Dwelling
Hungry	Starving, Ravenous, Famished, Voracious
Desire	Passion, Longing, Wanting, Yearning, Covet, Crave, Desiderate, Urge

Teeth	Glass, Enamel, Bone, Concrete
Embarrassed	Bashful, Humiliated, Ashamed, Warm, Flushed, Abashed
Shy	Bashful, Ashamed, Introvert, Demure, Meek, Timid, Coy, Diffident, Modest, Self effacing, Unassertive, Un-assured
Hear	Eaves drop, Noise, Attend, Hark, Hearken, Heed

Thirsty	Parched, Dried out, Dry mouth, Desire, Need a drink, Crave, Long for, Yearning, Hankering, Athirst, Thirsting
Priest (Catholic)	Father, Padre
Voice	Vocalize, Voicing, Sound, Verbalize
Frog	Toad, Tadpole

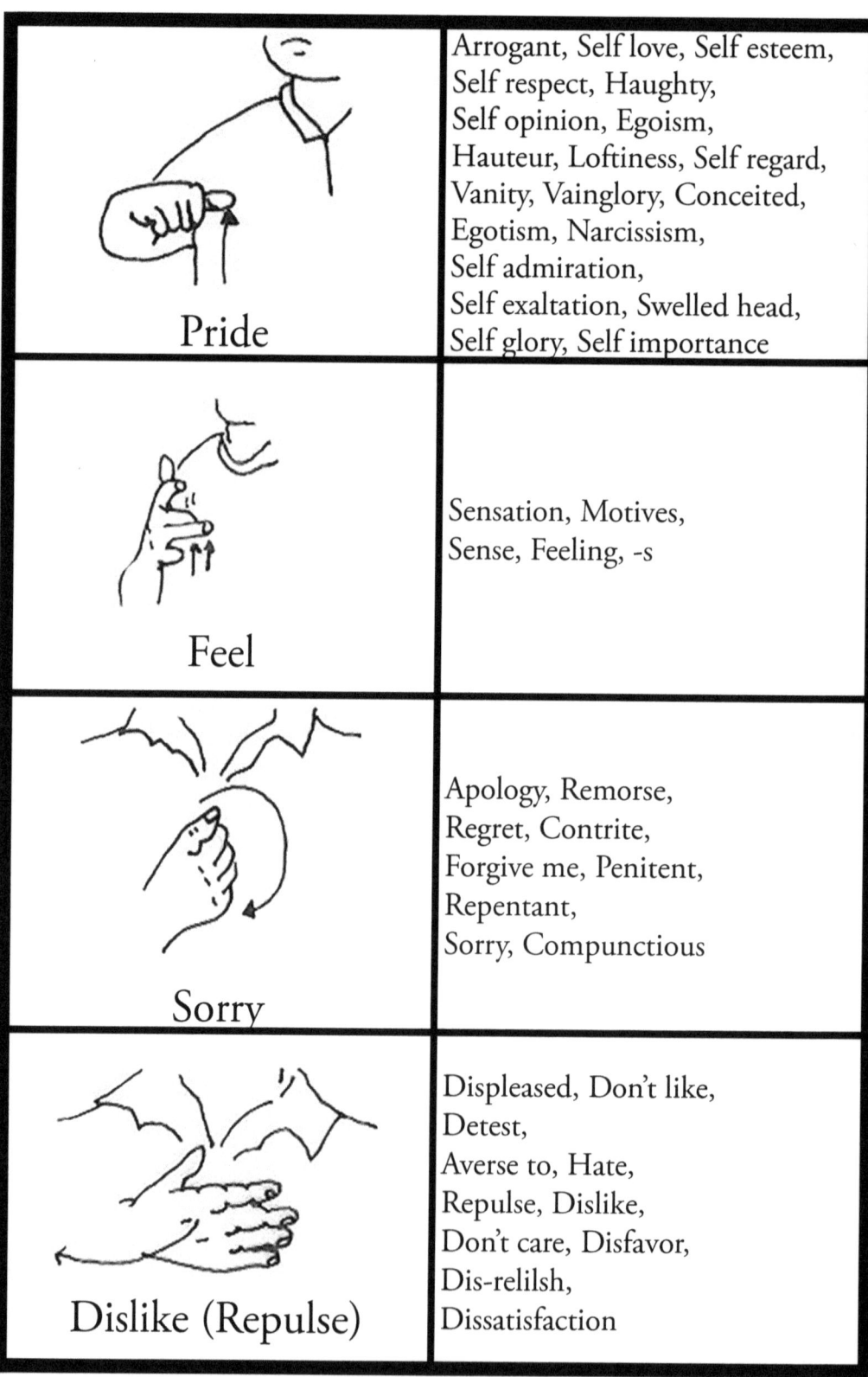

Pride	Arrogant, Self love, Self esteem, Self respect, Haughty, Self opinion, Egoism, Hauteur, Loftiness, Self regard, Vanity, Vainglory, Conceited, Egotism, Narcissism, Self admiration, Self exaltation, Swelled head, Self glory, Self importance
Feel	Sensation, Motives, Sense, Feeling, -s
Sorry	Apology, Remorse, Regret, Contrite, Forgive me, Penitent, Repentant, Sorry, Compunctious
Dislike (Repulse)	Displeased, Don't like, Detest, Averse to, Hate, Repulse, Dislike, Don't care, Disfavor, Dis-relilsh, Dissatisfaction

Bee	Gnat
Gold	Golden, California
Secretary	Assistant, Office, Support, Take Minutes, Clerk, Record keeper, Receptionist
Gum	Chewing gum, Bubble gum

Canada	Canadian, Canook
Bath	Tub, Bathe, Wash
Army	Military, Soldier
Boast	Puff up, Vaunt, Crow, Gasconade, Prate

Please	Pleasure, Take joy in, Gratify, Pleasurable, Relish, Delight, Delectable, Gladden, Happily, Voluptuous
Our	Ours
Refuse	Won't, Reject, Resist, Decline, Reprobate, Withhold, Disallow, Keep back
Rebel	Rebellious, Revolt, Mutiny, Anarchist, Insurrect, malcontent, Mutineer, Rice against, Revolutionary

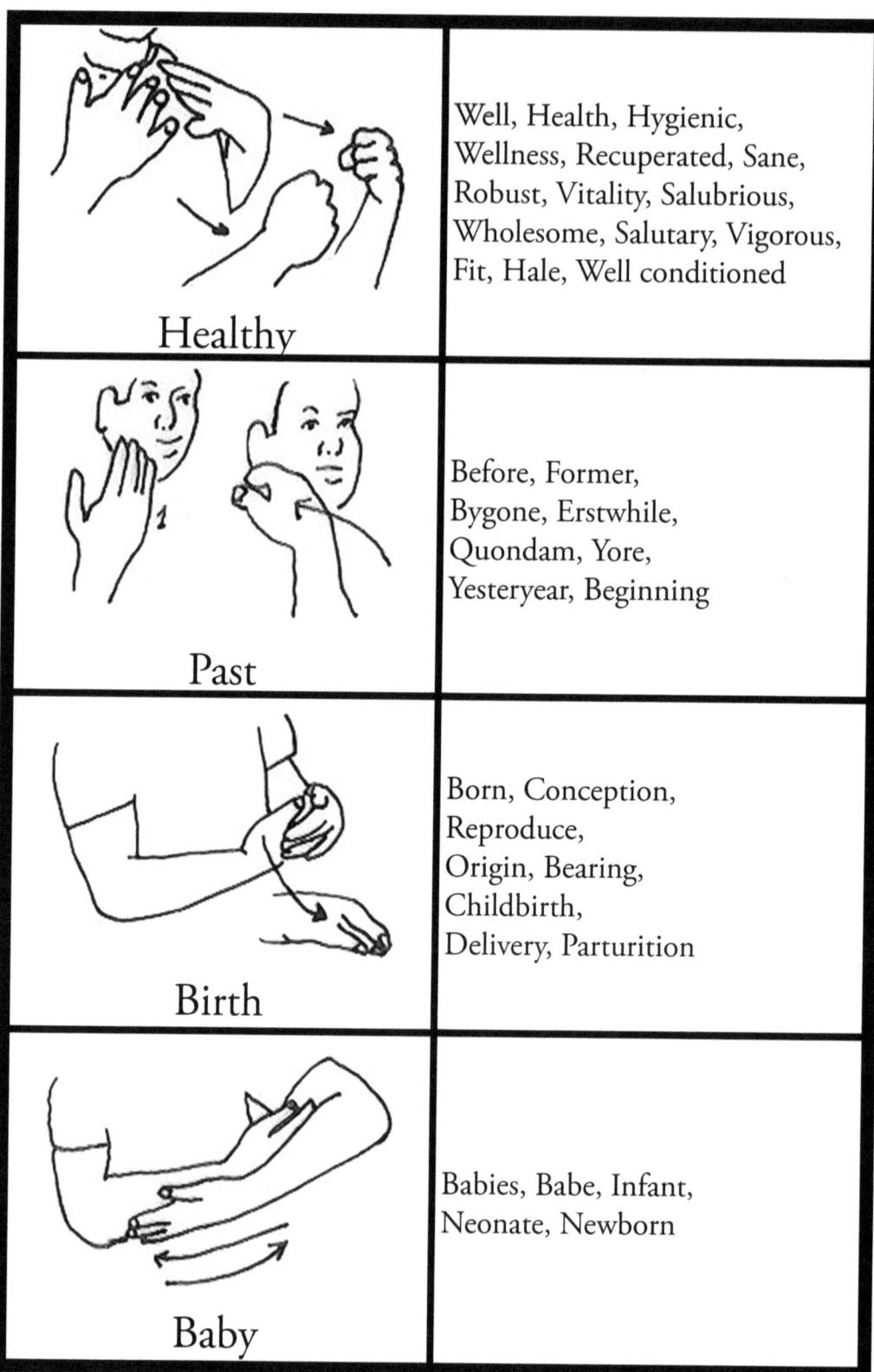

Healthy	Well, Health, Hygienic, Wellness, Recuperated, Sane, Robust, Vitality, Salubrious, Wholesome, Salutary, Vigorous, Fit, Hale, Well conditioned
Past	Before, Former, Bygone, Erstwhile, Quondam, Yore, Yesteryear, Beginning
Birth	Born, Conception, Reproduce, Origin, Bearing, Childbirth, Delivery, Parturition
Baby	Babies, Babe, Infant, Neonate, Newborn

Love	Adore, Cherish, To hold dear, Affection, Tender, Attachment, Devotion, Fondness, Amour, Passion
Happy	Glad, Exuberant, Joyful, Joyous, Lighthearted, Benevolent
Joy	Joyful, Glad, Pleasure, Delectation, Delight, Enjoyment, Fruition, Joyance
Like	Desire, Fancy, Enjoy, Relish, Interest

Pants	Trousers, Slacks, Jeans
Skirt	Skirts, Kilts, Lava lava
Tired	Exhausted, Sleepy, fatigued, Pooped, Weary, Fed up, Disgusted, Jaded, Worn out
Animal	Creature, Critter

Burden	Load, Weight, Charge, Deadweight, Duty, Millstone, Onus, Task, Tax, Encumber
Angel	Angels, Archangel, Celestial being, Heavenly being, Convince, Seraphim, cherubim, Cherub
Snow	Snowfall, Snowflake
Satisfied	Contented, Gratified, Appeased, Convinced, Filled, Fulfilled, Assured, Persuaded, Suited

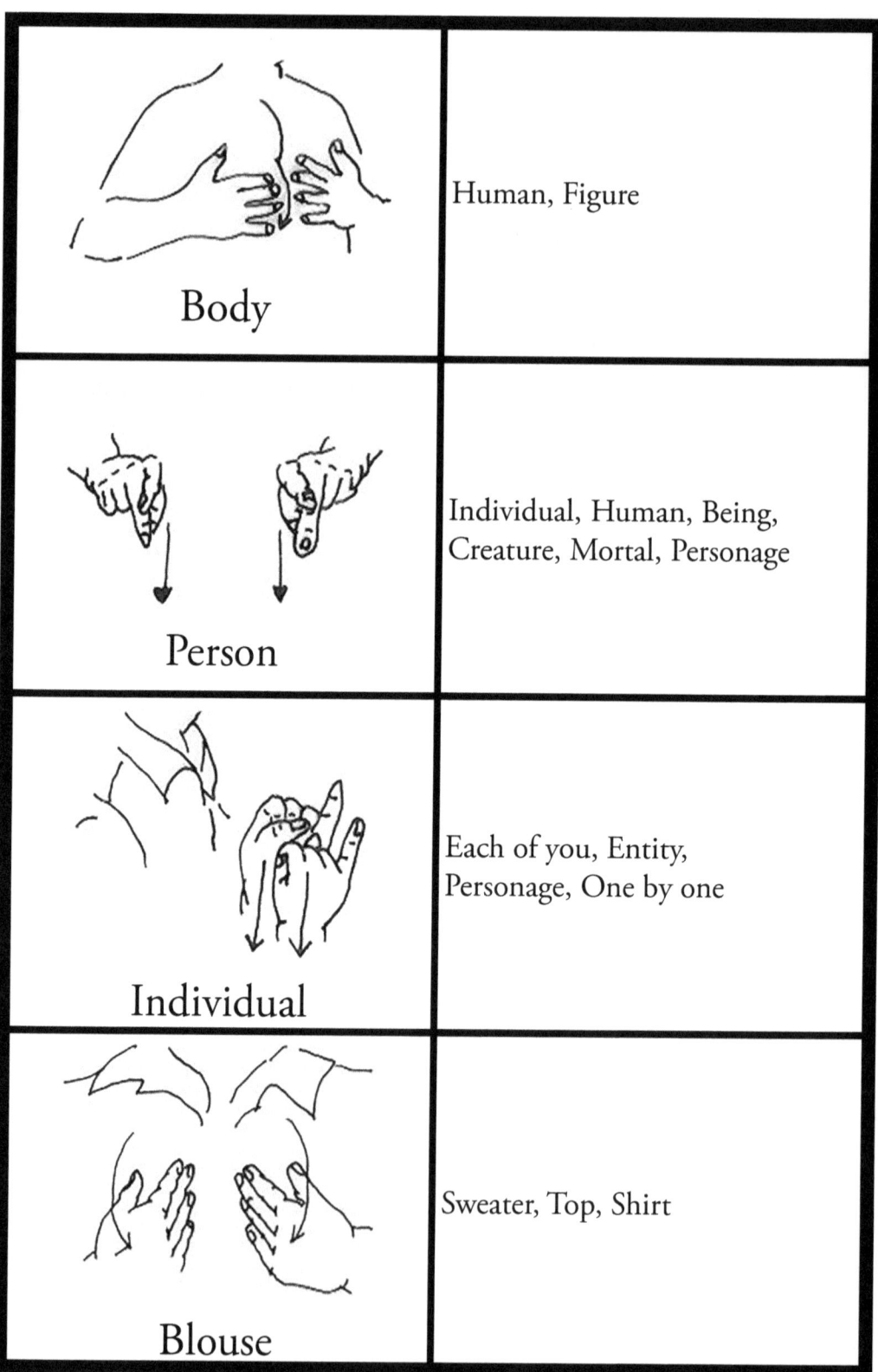

Body	Human, Figure
Person	Individual, Human, Being, Creature, Mortal, Personage
Individual	Each of you, Entity, Personage, One by one
Blouse	Sweater, Top, Shirt

Afraid	Frightened, Aghast, Anxious, Fearful, Terrified, Alarmed, Apprehensive, Phobia, Timid, Horror Nervous, Creeps, Terror, Cringe,
Have (to possess)	Possess, Own, Has, Had
Have (to finish)	Complete, End, Already, Done, Has, Had
Responsibility	Responsible, Reliable, Duty, Accountability, Amenable, Answerable, Liability, Border load

Enjoy	Please, Relish, Delight
Rude	Crude, coarse, Crass, Gross, Disrespectful, Ill Bread, Ill mannered, Uncivil, Impertinent, Impolite, Ungracious, Unrefined, Manner-less, Uncouth
Polite	Civil, Mannerly, Courteous, Gallant, Refined, Genteel, Well mannered
Fine	Well, Content, OK

Receive	Acceptance, Reception, Admission, Absorb, Acquire
Russia	Russian
Vacation	Retire, Take off, Holiday, Time off, Leave
Brave	Valiant, Valor, Bold, Undaunted, Gallant, Heroic, Audacity, Rash, Chivalry, Manliness, Grit, Mettle, Courageous, Guts, Spunk Spirit, Fearless, Intrepid, Un-fearful, Unafraid,

Performance	Act, Play, Perform, Opera
Complain	Gripe, Lament, Fuss, Murmur, Repine, Wail, Whine
Captain	Head, Chief, Commander, Counselor, Boss
Pittsburgh	Steel City

Elegant	Elegance, Refined, Polished, Fancy, Exquisite, Rare
Clothes	Apparel, Attire, Duds, Garments, Habiliments, Raiment, Grab
Dress	Clothes
Accept	Adopt, Admit

Volunteer	Enlist, Available, Willing
Alone	By yourself, Single, Separate, Only, Apart, Detached, Isolated, Removed, Unaccompanied, Solitary, Lone, Sole, Singular, Solo
We	Us
Since	From that time, Ago, Subsequently, In as much as, Because

Kingdom	Domain
Lord	Master, Ruler, Noble
Lazy	Passive, Indolent, Slothful, Idle, Laze, Loaf, Lunge, Vegetate, Bum
Personality	Character, Individuality, Deposition, Makeup, Nature, Temperament

Police	Cops, Vigilantes, Policeman, Bluecoat, Gumshoe, John Law, Officer, Patrolman, Peace officer
Religion	Denomination, Creed, Faith, Persuasion, Sect
Member	Constituent, Fellow, Partner, Affiliation
Feeling	Emotion, Sensation, Experience, Passion, Sentient, Affection, Sentimental, Conviction, Sense, Sensation, Sensitivity

Heart	Center, Care, Core, Root
King	Head of, Ruler, Monarch, Royalty, Emperor, Sovereign, Magnate, Baron, Mogul, Czar
Queen	Ruler, Monarch, Royalty, Sovereign
Prince	Princess, Magnate, Baron, Baroness

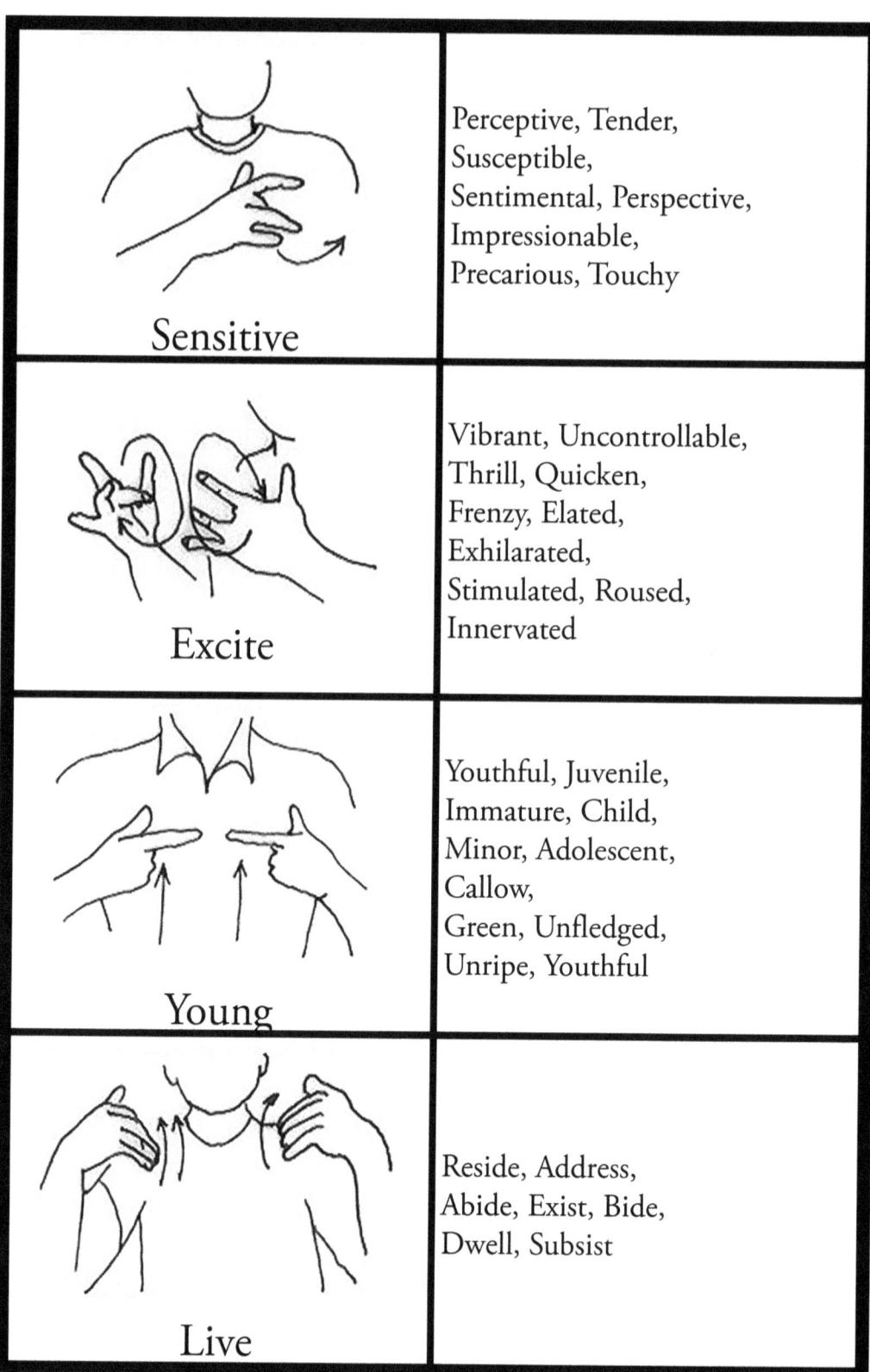

Sensitive	Perceptive, Tender, Susceptible, Sentimental, Perspective, Impressionable, Precarious, Touchy
Excite	Vibrant, Uncontrollable, Thrill, Quicken, Frenzy, Elated, Exhilarated, Stimulated, Roused, Innervated
Young	Youthful, Juvenile, Immature, Child, Minor, Adolescent, Callow, Green, Unfledged, Unripe, Youthful
Live	Reside, Address, Abide, Exist, Bide, Dwell, Subsist

Poor	Indignant, Unsatisfactory, Imperfect, Beggared, Broke, Flimsy, Penny-less, Destitute, Dirt poor, Flat broke, Fortuneless, Needy, Impecunious, Penurious, Impoverished, Necessitous, Poverty Stricken, Stone broke, Strapped, Un-prosperous
Force	Power, Mighty, make, Coerce, Compel, Concuss, constrain
Punish	Rebuke, Reprove, Castigate, Chasten, Chastise, Correct, Discipline, Consequence
Long	Extended, Lengthy, Elongated, Tedious

 Sheep	Lamb, Ewe, Kid
 Steal	Take, Apprehend, Thievery, Rob, Theft, Larceny, Loot, Lift, Pinch, Purloining, Abduct, Burglarize, Snatch
 Bridge	Crossover, Span, Viaduct, Undercross
 Temptation	Coercion, Persuasion, Enticement, Snare, Allure, -ment, Bait, Lure, Come on, Decoy, Inveiglement, Seducement, Siren Song, Snare

Thin	Lean, Slender, Narrow, Attenuate, Reedy, Slight, Slim, Skinny, Tenuous, Fine
Hospital	Clinic
Fall (Season)	Autumn
Country	Land, Region, Homeland, Rural, Fatherland, Motherland

Lock	Secure, Fasten, Close
Defeat	Beat, Overpower, Rout, Blast, Crush, Dust, Lick, Curry, Thrash, Drub, Prevail, Lambaste, Mop up, Triumph, Skunk, Whip, Overrun, Overcome, Upend, Overwhelm, Shellac, Trounce, Smother, Steam roll, Wallop, Whomp, Control
Establish	Found, Start, Root, Build, Foundation, Confirm, Secure, Set up, Install Institute, Create, Constitute, Organize
Improve	Advance, Ascent, Build up, Develop, Enhance, Promotion, Progress, Perk up, Make better, Ameliorate, Convalesce, Grain, Look up, Mend, Recuperate

Rock	Pebble, Foundation, Boulder, Stone, Pebble
Mountain	Cliff, Hill, Peak, Alp, Mount
Church	Chapel, House of Worship, House of God, House of prayer, Tabernacle, Temple, Place of Worship
Temple	Pagoda, Synagogue, Church, House of God, House of Worship, House of prayer, Mosque

Work	Drudgery, Grind, Labor, Toil, Job, Trade, Employment, Occupation, Pursuit, Operate, Function
Busy	Active, Business, Firm, Hard work, Industry, -ing, Livelihood, In use, Engrossed, Concern, Occupied, Establishment, Bustling, Function, Hustling, Duty, Province,
Fin	Acquisition, Come across, Discover, Detect, -ing, -ound, Locate, Espial, Strike, Spot, Encounter, Hit on
Engaged	Betrothed, Espoused, Intended, Affianced

Deteriorate	Decline, Lessen, Degenerate, Dis-improve, Disintegrate, Retrograde, Sink, Worsen, Digress
Slow	Creep, Crawl, Leisurely, Dilatory, Retardation, Stroll, Plod, Trudge, Laggard, Un-hasty, Unhurried
Sing	Carol, Chant, Harmony, Melody, Melodic, Music, Song
Blame	Accuse, Fault, Cause, Condemn, -ation, Criticism, Culpability, Denunciation, Onus, Rap, reprove, Reprehensible

Time	Duration, Period, Span, Space, Spell
Duty	Commitment, Commission, Charge, Liability, Onus, Obligation, Task, Responsibility, Assignment Devoir
Nurse	Medical Attendant, R.N., L.V.N
Doctor	Chiropractor, Consultant, Physician, Surgeon, M.D., Holder of Doctoral degree, General Practitioner, Medico

 Potato	Spud, Tater
 Whiskey	Liquor, Moonshine, Booze, Hooch, Alcoholic beverage
 Naked	Empty, Nothing on, Nude, Unclad, Honed, Undressed, Keen, Au natural, Bluff, Acute, Raw, Stripped, Wetted, Acute, Birthday suit, Sharp, Vacant
 Bald	Bare headed, Baldly, Hairless, Glabrous, Smooth headed, Naked head, Vacant

Earth	Globe, Planet, Sphere, Terrestrial, Orb, World
Touch	Caress, Contact, Pat, Stroke, Tap, Finger, Handle, Palpate, Paw, Tactility
Most	Approximately, Nearly all, Practically all, "Superlative degree of an adjective"
Lost	Absent, Can't find, Disappeared, Gone, Not here, Lacking, Omitted, Missing

Dive	Leap, Plunge, Jump, Lunge
Island	Isle
Institution	Asylum, Company, Residential School, Institute, Organization
Advice	Affect, Counsel, Guidance, Suggestion, Recommendation, Influence

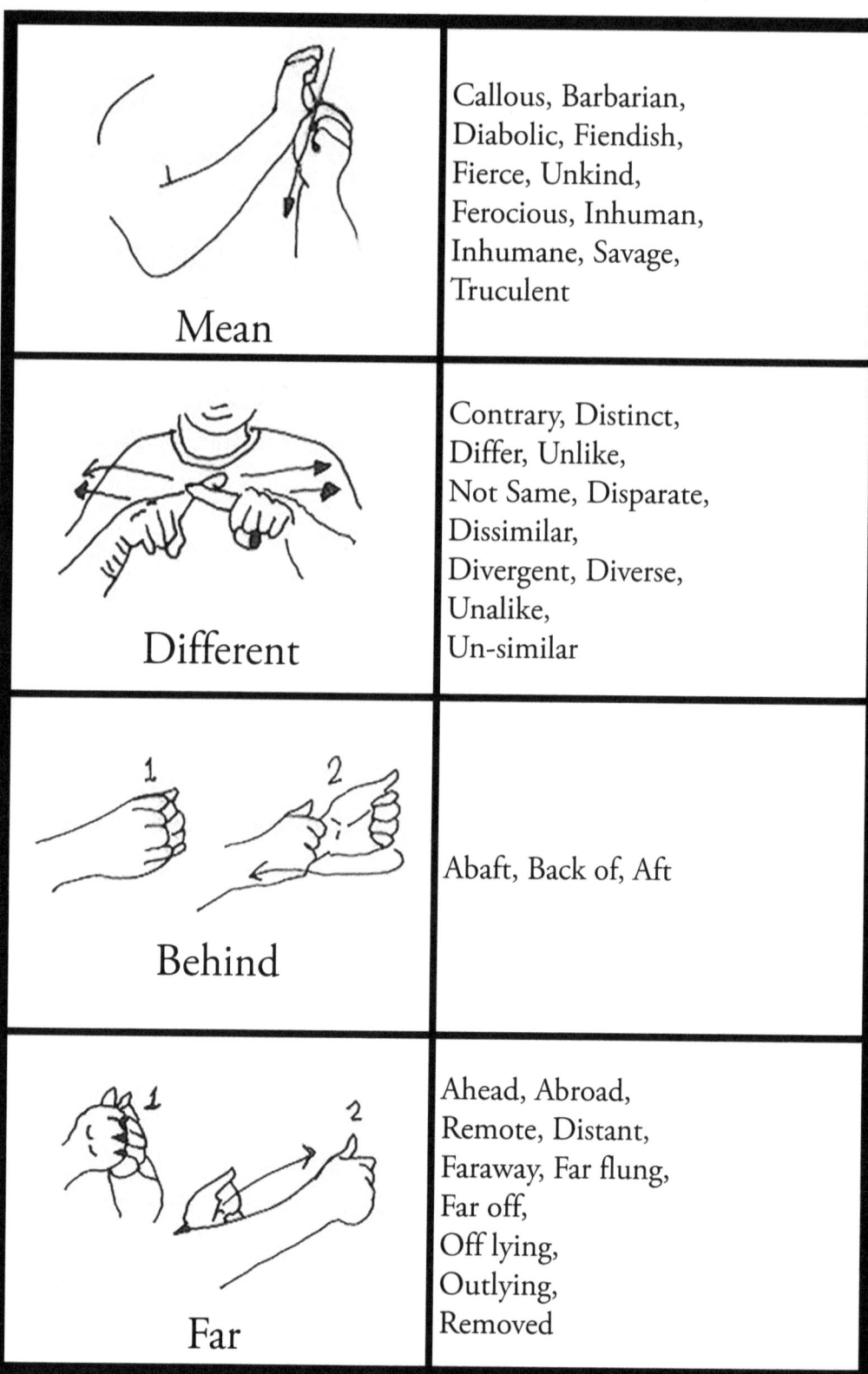

Mean

Callous, Barbarian, Diabolic, Fiendish, Fierce, Unkind, Ferocious, Inhuman, Inhumane, Savage, Truculent

Different

Contrary, Distinct, Differ, Unlike, Not Same, Disparate, Dissimilar, Divergent, Diverse, Unalike, Un-similar

Behind

Abaft, Back of, Aft

Far

Ahead, Abroad, Remote, Distant, Faraway, Far flung, Far off, Off lying, Outlying, Removed

Ever	Each one, Every one
Chase	Trail, Ensue, Follow, Chivy, Pursue
Catch	Caught up, Not behind
Help	Aid, Assist, -ant, Helper, Lend a hand

Support	Advocate, In favor of, Supporting, Back, Side with, Bolster, Sustain
Assistant	Aid, Aide, Attendant, Helper
Full	Chock-full, Packed, Brimful, Awash, Brimming, Cram-full, Crammed, Jammed, Replete, Stuffed, Fed up, Laden, Voluminous
Enough	Adequate, Plenty, Sufficient

Coffee	Joe, Caf, Java
Wash	Clean, Cleanse, Lave, Scrub
Year	Yearly, Once a year, Annual
Backslide	Backslidden, Fall behind, Lapse, Recidivate, Relapse

Holy	Clean, Hallowed, Consecrated, Sacred, Sanctified, Un-profane
Nice	Pleasant, Agreeable, Congenial, Favorable
Clean	Kept, Spotless, Tidy, Immaculate, Modest, Stainless, Unblemished, Undefiled, Unsullied, Taintless, Unsoiled
Gone	Disappear, -ed, Missing, Went, Vanished, Bygone, Away, Lacking, Omitted, Empty

Operation	Surgery, Incision, Scar
Remove	Deduct, Eliminate, Get rid of, Subtract, Liquidate
Iron	Ferric, Ferrous, Metal, Metallic, Oxide
Practice	Drill, Repeat, Rehearsal

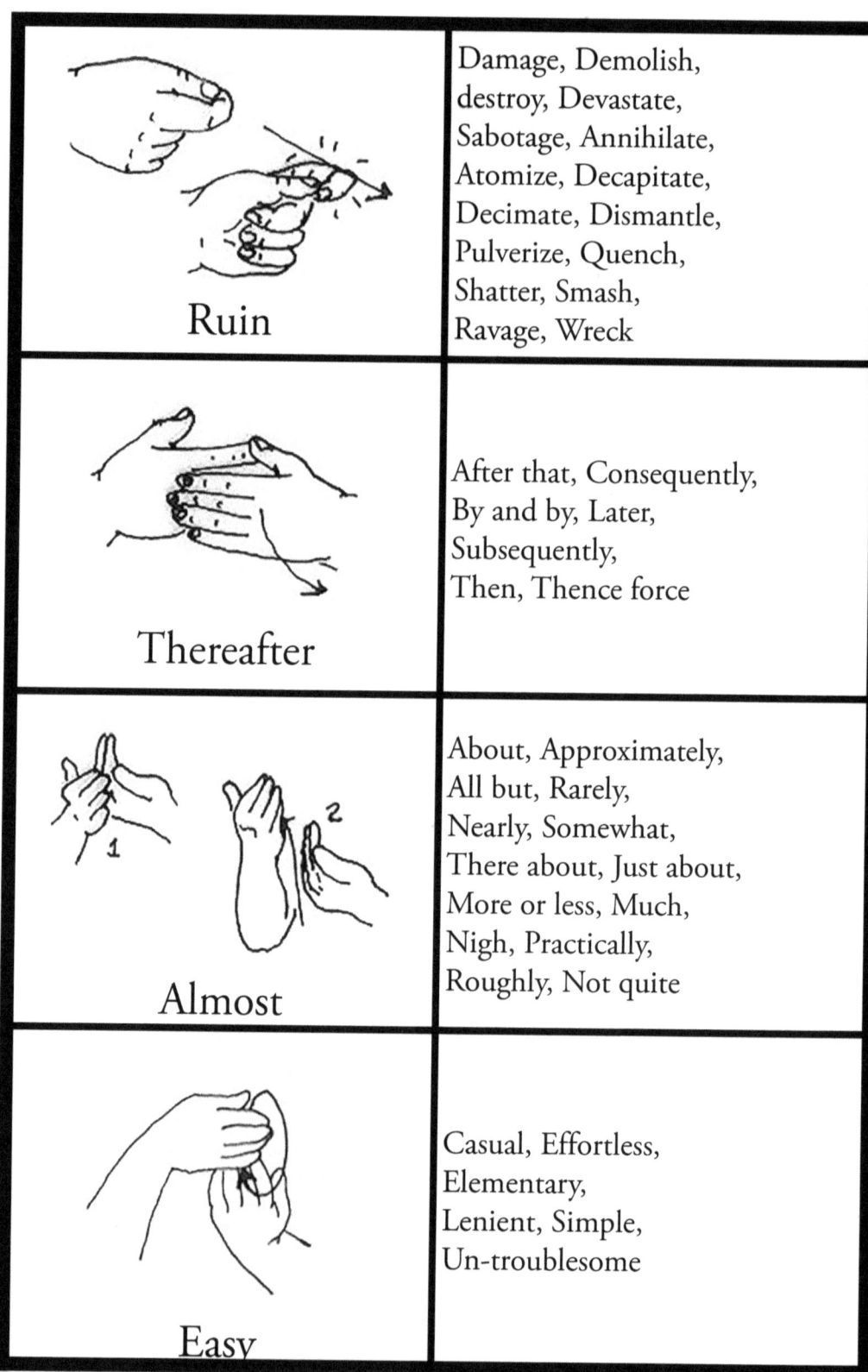

Ruin	Damage, Demolish, destroy, Devastate, Sabotage, Annihilate, Atomize, Decapitate, Decimate, Dismantle, Pulverize, Quench, Shatter, Smash, Ravage, Wreck
Thereafter	After that, Consequently, By and by, Later, Subsequently, Then, Thence force
Almost	About, Approximately, All but, Rarely, Nearly, Somewhat, There about, Just about, More or less, Much, Nigh, Practically, Roughly, Not quite
Easy	Casual, Effortless, Elementary, Lenient, Simple, Un-troublesome

First	Foremost, Headmost, Inaugural, Initial, Leading, Original, Primary, Prime
Spirit	Ghost, Apparition, Bogey, Phantasm, Phantom, Revenant, Specter, Umbra, Wraith
Holy Spirit	Comforter, Holy Ghost
Spoil-pet too much	Coddle, Pamper, Cater to, Cosset, Cotton, Humor, Indulge

	Today
Day	
	Daybreak, Daylight, Dawn, Before noon, Forenoon, Sunup, Sunrise, Morn, Aurora
Morning	
	Evening, Last night, Sunset, Tonight, Twilight, Nighttime, Night tide, Nocturnal
Night	
	12 P.M. Witching hour
Midnight	

Sandwich	Snack
Forgive	Absolve, Excuse, Exempt, Pardon, Waive, Condone, Remit
Excuse	Exempt, Forgive, Pardon, Waive, Condon, Remit, Alibi, Plea, Pretext
Fired	Canned, Discharged, Dismissed, Let go, Sent packing, Terminated, Axed, Booted out, Sacked

New	Clean, Current, Fresh, Original, Untouched, Modern, Novel, Neoteric, Newfangled, Anew, Renewed, Refreshed, Revived
Print	Publish, News paper, Writing
Paper	Stationary, Essay, Composition, Theme
Part	Component, Element, Fraction, Fragment, Portion, Piece, Share, Partition, Segment, Some, Not all, Lot, Ration, Allotment, Allowance, Quota, Part

Noon	High noon, Midday, Noontime
Slice	Cut, Piece, Portion, Thin piece, Section, Sharing, Wedge, Carve, Cleave, Dissect, Disserve
Bread	Loaf
Cheap	Bargain, Economical, Low cost, Low price, Inexpensive, Reasonable, Un-costly, Cheesy, Paltry, Shabby, Scummy, Shoddy, Sleazy, Trashy, Trumpery

Some	Element, Part, Piece Portion, Selection, Segment, Not all, Nearly, All but, Approximately, Just about, More or less
Soap	Cleanser, Detergent, Lather soap
Encourage	Advocate, Boost, Edify, Promote, Animate, Cheer, Embolden, Nerve Steel, Strengthen, In favor of, Uplift
Plow	Cultivate, Break, Till, To farm, Turn over, Harrow

Anyway	Anyhow, Doesn't matter, Even though, Regardless, In spite of, In any case, In any event, Whatever, Nevertheless, No matter, Anywise
Wood	Log, Timber, Wooden
Arrive	Arrived, Get to, Get there, Land, Reach
Again	Encore, Repeat, Over, Afresh, Anew, De novo, Once more, One more time, Over & Over

Often	Again and again, Constantly, Oftentimes, Regularly, Frequently, Much many times, More than once, Oft, Recurrently, Repeatedly, Over and over, Time and again
Tree	Forest, Trees, Timber, Woods, Woodland
Flag	Banner, Banderole, Bannerol, Burgee, Ensign, Pendant, Pennant, Standard, Streamer
Cheese	Curds

Across	Cross, Thwart, Beyond, crosswise, Crossways, Cross over, Transversely, Over
All	Every, Entirely, Total, -ly, Inclusive, Whole, All in all, Altogether, In toto, Complete, Include
All right	Allowed, Fine, Permitted, OK
Fast	Pronto, Rapid, Right away, Speedily, Full tilt, Suddenly, Swift, Immediately, Promptly Fleet Breakneck, Expeditious, Hastily, Post Haste, Snappy, Chop chop, Presto,

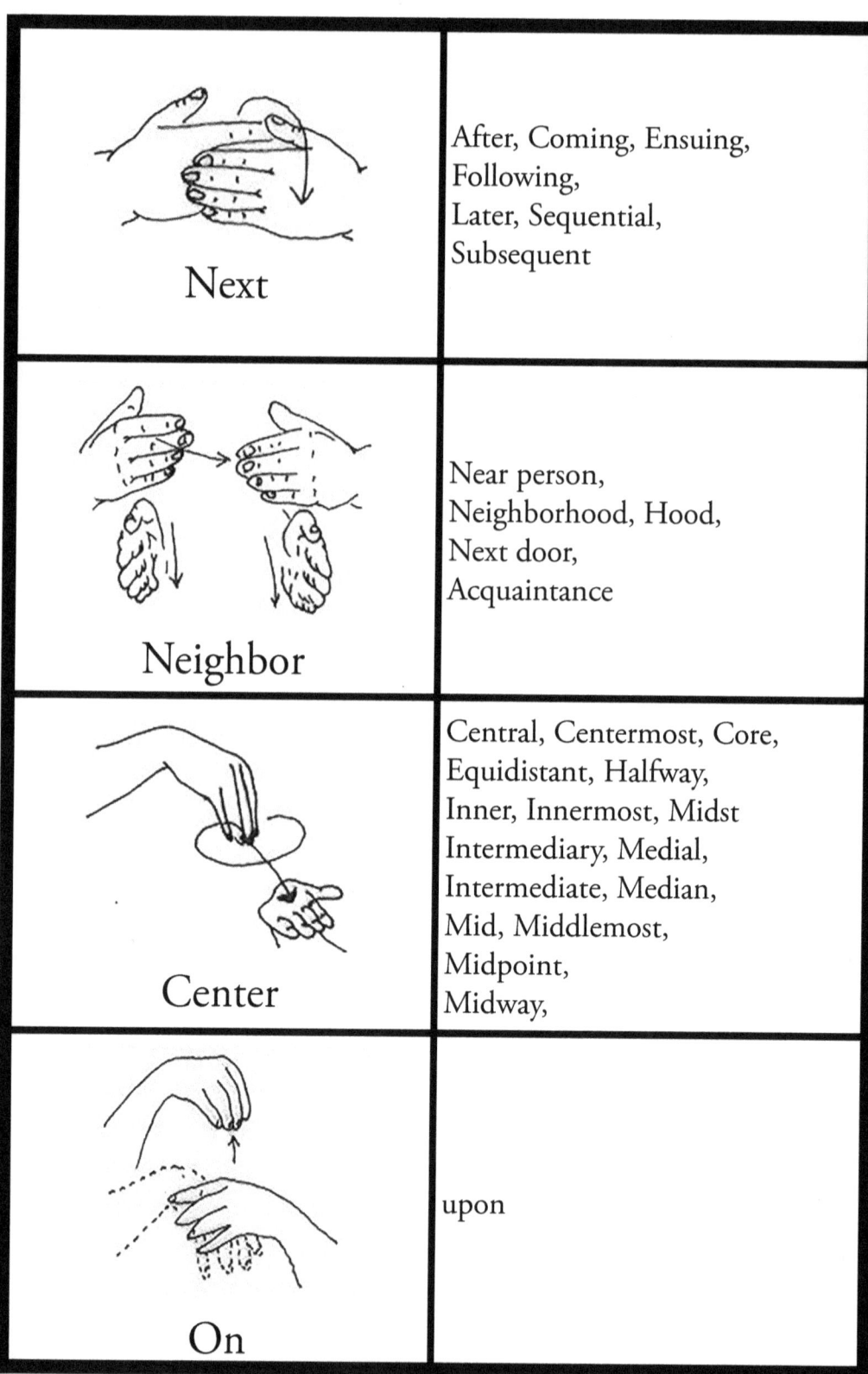

Next	After, Coming, Ensuing, Following, Later, Sequential, Subsequent
Neighbor	Near person, Neighborhood, Hood, Next door, Acquaintance
Center	Central, Centermost, Core, Equidistant, Halfway, Inner, Innermost, Midst Intermediary, Medial, Intermediate, Median, Mid, Middlemost, Midpoint, Midway,
On	upon

Jail	Detention, Bars, Coop, Incarceration, Imprison, -ment, Penitentiary, Bastille, Confinement, Constrain, Immure, Jug, Intern, Brig, Cooler, Pen, Guardroom, Lockup, Reformatory, Slammer, Stockade
Fence	Coop, Corral, Hedge, Hem, Immure, Pen
Door	Entrance, Gate, Entranceway, Portal
Open	Ajar, Begin, Patient, Unclosed, Unobstructed, Unrestricted, Passage

Close	Shut, Slam
Gate	Hinge, Fence opening
Near	Almost, Approach, Close by, Close to, Neighborhood, Next to, Near at hand, Nearby, Nigh Toward
Retaliate	Avenge, Get even, Revenge, Reciprocate, recompense, Requite, Vindicate

In	Internal, Inner, Inside
Out	Outside, Leave, Get out, Go out
Resign	Back out, Drop out, Quit, Withdraw, Step down, relinquish, Abandon, Cede, Yield, Demit, Abdicate, Renounce
Lesson	Course, Chapter, Section, Exercise

Nag	Complain, Grumble, Hen peck, Carp at, Fuss at, Pick on
Money	Finances, Fund, cash, Currency, Sough, Filthy Lucre, Legal tender, Loot, Lucre, Stuff, Pelf, Swag, Capital
School	Learning Institution, Educational Institution
High School	Learning Institution, Secondary School

Warm	Alert, Admonish, Reprove, Call out, Caution, Forewarn
Call	Summon, Call in
Invite	Hire, Invitation, Usher, Welcome, Bid
Weak	Feeble, Flimsy, Fragile, Frail, Insubstantial, Puny, Unsound, Weary, Wobbly, Fatigue

Lear	Acquire knowledge, Educate
Study	Concentrate, Practice, Rehearse
Copy	Duplicate, Imitate, Mimic, Model, Reproduce, Carbon, Ditto, Facsimile, Republication, Replica, Replicate, Replication
Cancel	Annul, Call off, Drop plan, Delete, Condemn, Correct, Criticize, Cross out, Find fault

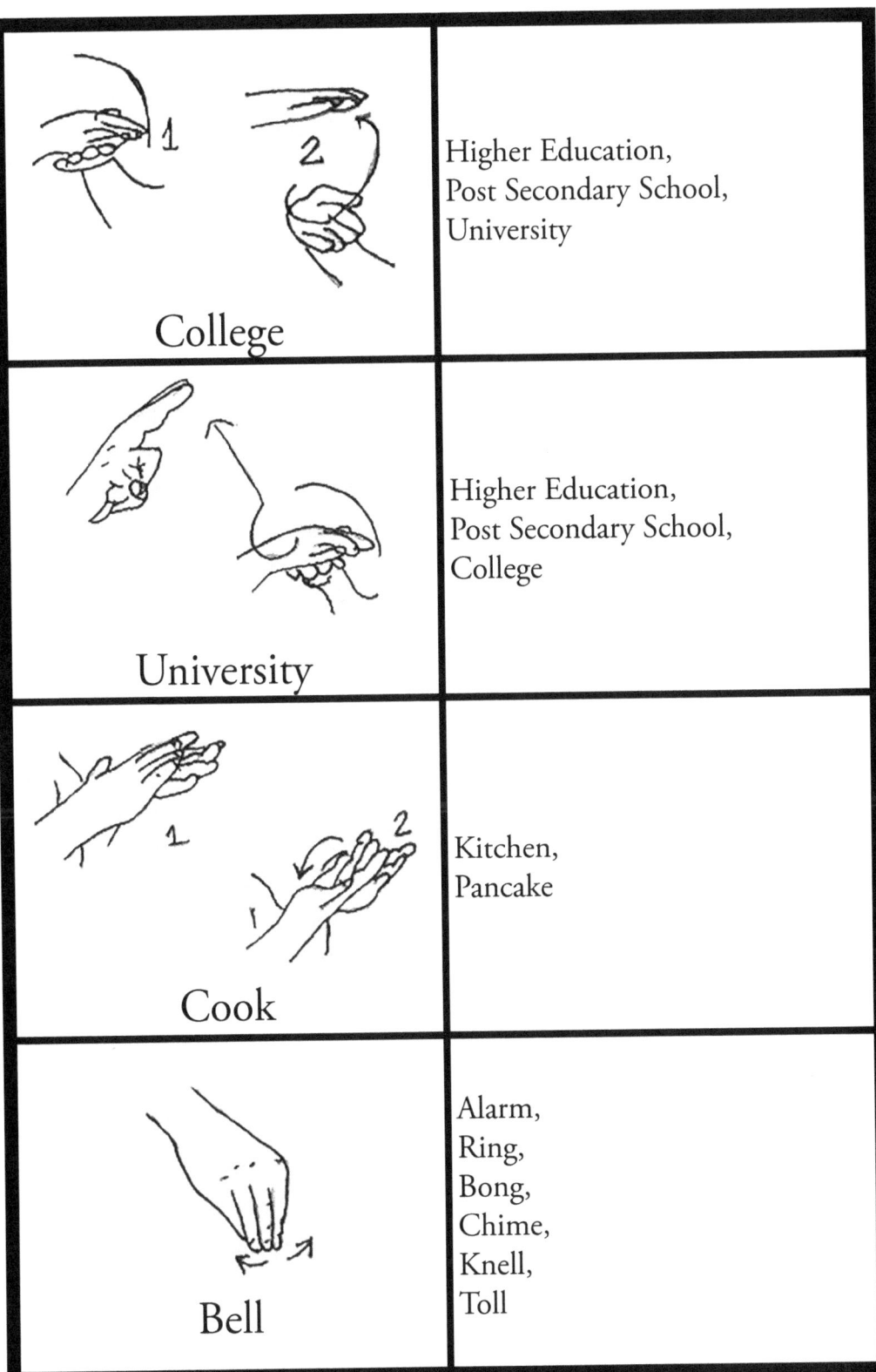

College	Higher Education, Post Secondary School, University
University	Higher Education, Post Secondary School, College
Cook	Kitchen, Pancake
Bell	Alarm, Ring, Bong, Chime, Knell, Toll

Boil	Babble, Cook, Heat, Bristle, Flare up, Seethe, Churn, Ferment, Simmer, Smolder, Stew, Parboil
Fire	Burn, Flame, Inferno, Blaze
Hell	Burn forever, Abyss, Blazes, Gahanna, Hades, Inferno, Netherworld, Pit, Sheol, Lake of fire
Glory	Glorious, Exult, Jubilate, Exalt, Glorify, Praise, Worship

Skill	Able, Ability, Agile, Capable, Efficient, Enable, Expertise, Hardy, Talent, Knack, Expertness, Know how, Mastership, Mastery, Dexterity, Deftness, Adroitness
Count	Counted, Counting, Enumerate, Tale, Tally, Figure out, Number
Accountant	Book keeper, Financial advisor
Meat	Beef, Skin, Steak, Flesh

Tall	Big, High, Height, Altitudinous
Deep	Depth, Detail, Abysmal, Profound
Kill	Murder, Slay, Slaughter, Carry off, Finish, Take out, Snuff
What	What for?, What's up?, Huh?, Whatever

Earn	Accountable, Collect, -ion, Reap, Deserve, Gather, Income, Salary, Wage, Acquire, Bring in, Draw in, Gain, Get, Merit
Picture	Photo, Photograph, Image, Portrait, Simulacrum
Glass	Can, Mug, Stein Vessel
Biscuit	Cookie, Cake, Dumpling, Roll

What	What for?, What's up?, Huh?, Whatever
Situation	State, Condition, Mode, Posture, Status, Surrounding
Minute	Just a minute, Moment, -arily, Instant, Flash, Jiffy, Shake, Twinkle, Wink
Hour	One hour, 60 minutes

Butter	Margarine, Oleo
Honest	Frank, -ly, Honesty, Respect, Sincere, Sure, Genuine, true, Upright, Just, Right, Conscientious, Scrupulous
Welding	Solder, Fusing metals, Brazing, Glue Gun
Draw	Design, Draft, Drawing, Art, Color

Party	Celebration, Social, Gathering
Verse	Scripture, Stanza
Late	Not yet, Tardy, Not done, Delayed, Behind, Belated, Overdue, Unpunctual
During	While, As, Meanwhile, Mean time, Amid, Thorough out, Midst

Snake	Reptile, Serpent, Viper
Worm	Caterpillar, Larva
Soda pop	Soft drink
Spoon	Soup

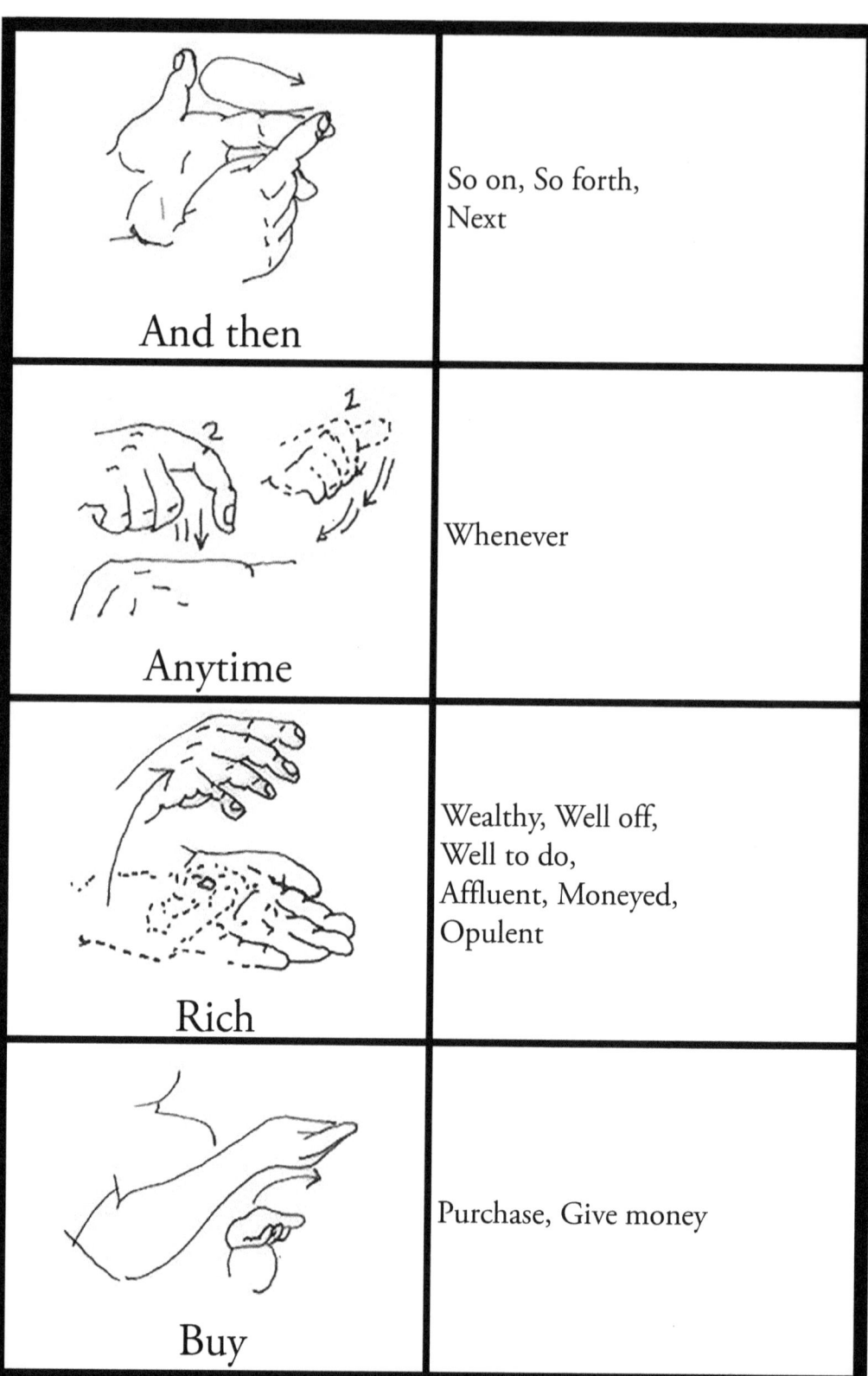

And then	So on, So forth, Next
Anytime	Whenever
Rich	Wealthy, Well off, Well to do, Affluent, Moneyed, Opulent
Buy	Purchase, Give money

Rise	Get up, Arise, Stand up, Upspring
Meaning	Imply, Intent, Motive, Intend, Purpose, Signify, Stand for, Design, Intent, Import, Aim, Connoting, Denoting
Ticket	Voucher, Claim check, Carte d' entrée, Fine
Write	Scribble, Jot down, Scribe, Correspond, Engross, Inscribe

Medicine	Drugs, Medication
Gravy	Grease
Through	Via, Passage, By way of
Escape	Get away, Runaway, Flee, Exit, Evade, Retreat, Bold, Bail out, Abscond, Break, Decamp Lam, Slip

Waste	Throw out, Throw away, Squander, Frivol away, Blow, Blunder away, Dissipate, Dribble, away, Fritter away, Muddle away, Trifle away
Expensive	Costly, High, Much money
Read	Skim
Fall down	Stumble, Trip

	Alpha, Start, Commence, Onset, Initiate, Embark on, Inaugurate, Kick off, Launch, Originate
Begin	
	Dwindle, Vanish, Disappear, Fade, Evaporate, Liquefy, Deliquesce, Flux, Evanesce, Biodegrade, Thaw, Vanish
Melt	
	Silky, Glazed, Polished, Sleek, Slick, Refine, Without problems
Smooth	
	With child, Expecting, Enceinte, Expectant, Parturient
Pregnant	

To	Toward, Goal
About	Around, Nearly, Almost, As good as, Approximately, Just about, More or less, Much, Nigh, Practically, Roughly, Roundly
Around	Surrounding, Neighboring, Round about, Circa, Close on, Nearby
Harvest	Reap, Gather, Collect, Earn, Garner, Ingather, Crop

Plant	Deposit, Sow, Seed
Place (to put)	Set, Lay, Stick
Monkey	Gorilla, Ape, Orangutan, Chimpanzee, Chimp
Bear	Grizzly, Panda, Teddy

Turtle	Tortoise
Hide	Cover up, Camouflage, Conceal, Ensconce, Stash
Fountain	Spring, Wellspring
Sew	Stitch, Mend

Bring	Carry, Convey, Transport
Plan	Budget, Animus, Arrange, Intend, Intention, Schedule, Scheme, Design
Boat	Barge, Vessel, Ferry, Canoe
Maybe	Possibly, Perhaps, Perchance, Conceivably, Possibly

River	Canal, Creek, Stream
Way	Mode, Passage, Path, Route, Style, Method, Fashion, Manner, Modus, Technique
Road	Street, Avenue, Alley, Lane, Blvd, Highway, Path, Way, Thoroughfare, Track, Sidewalk
Bury	Funeral, Entomb, Inhume, Sepulcher, Sepulture, Tomb

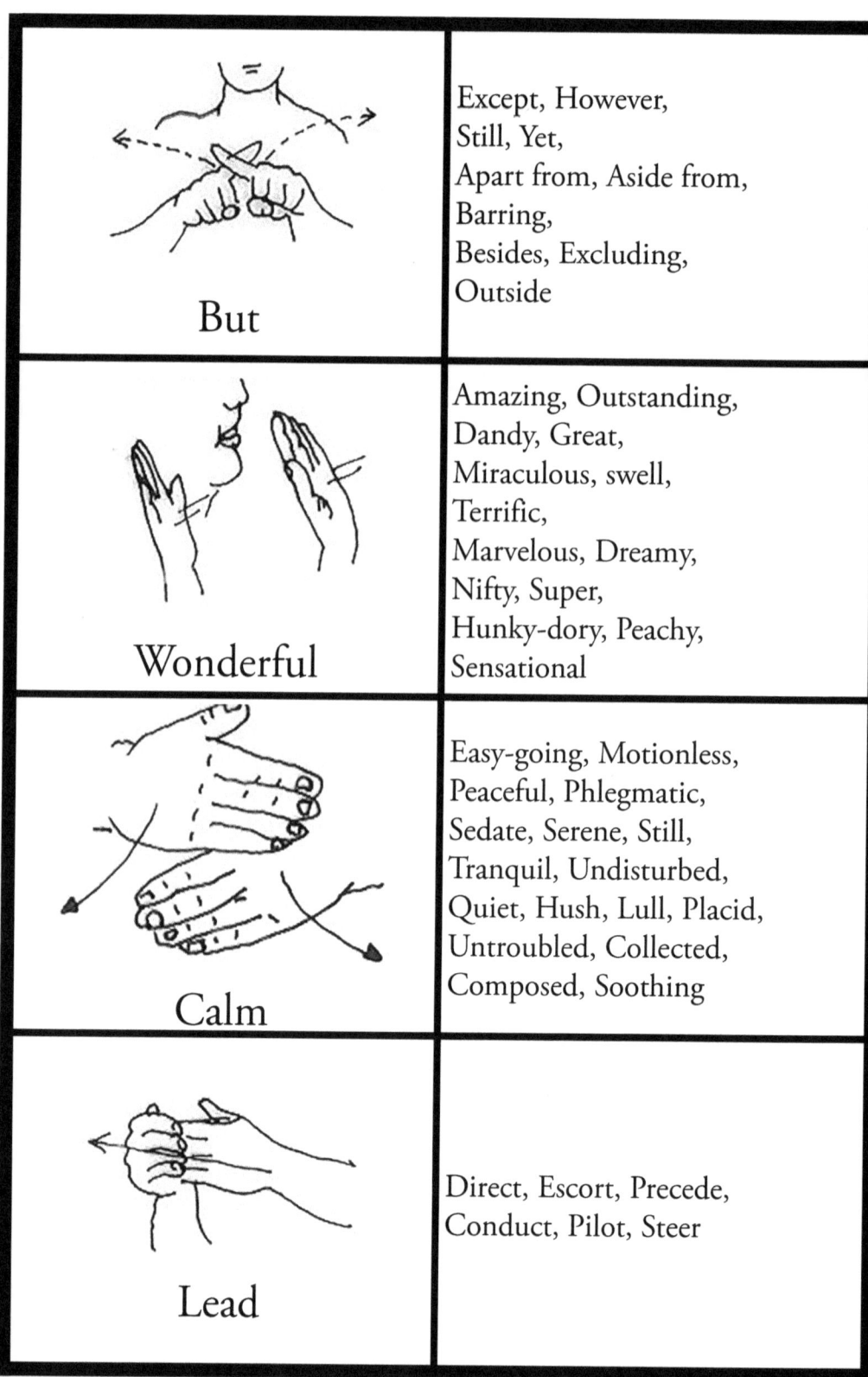

But

Except, However,
Still, Yet,
Apart from, Aside from,
Barring,
Besides, Excluding,
Outside

Wonderful

Amazing, Outstanding,
Dandy, Great,
Miraculous, swell,
Terrific,
Marvelous, Dreamy,
Nifty, Super,
Hunky-dory, Peachy,
Sensational

Calm

Easy-going, Motionless,
Peaceful, Phlegmatic,
Sedate, Serene, Still,
Tranquil, Undisturbed,
Quiet, Hush, Lull, Placid,
Untroubled, Collected,
Composed, Soothing

Lead

Direct, Escort, Precede,
Conduct, Pilot, Steer

Ignore	Disregard, Neglect, Overlook, Discount, Elide, Pass over, Slight
Trouble	Affliction, Problems, Distress, Trial
Worry	Troubled, Concerned, Fret, Disquiet, Uneasy, Distress, Un-restful, Disturbed, Anxious, Uneasy, Concern, Fuss
Ask	Request, Inquire, Pray, Bid, Bespeak, Solicit

Serve	Attend, Aide, Provide, Supply, Wait on, minister to, Trend
Leave (it there)	Abandon, Bequeath, Forgo, Forsake, Relinquish, Surrender, Cede, Waive, Place
Leave(depart)	Exit, Get away, Pull put, Push off, Shove off, Take off, Withdraw
Suggest	Offer, Bid, Extend, Present, Propose, Pose, Proffer, Tender

Stand	Pause, Remain, Upright
Dance	Ballet, Break dance, Dancing, Hop, Jazz, Tap dance, Prance
Funeral	Burial procession
Run	Gallop, Hasten, Barrel, Beeline, Bolt, Bustle, Flee, Flint, Fly, Hot foot, Scoot, Scamper, Scurry, Sprint, Skedaddle, Running, Ran, Zip

	English, Britain
England	
	Concerned, Eager, Agog, Appetent, Ardent, Avid, Impatient, Keen, Raring
Anxiou	
	At ease, Content, Cozy, Relaxed, Satisfied, Solaced, Comfy, cozy, cushy, Easeful, Snug
Comfortable	
	Chance, Gamble, Betting, Lay odds, Wager, Stake
Bet	

	Foot
Feet	
	Hike, Meander, Pace, Stroll, Tramp, Tread, Trod, Wander, Ambulate, Foot it, Hoof it, Step, Traipse, Troop, Ramble, Saunter
Walk	
	Parade
March	
	Bag, Baggage, Suitcase
Luggage	

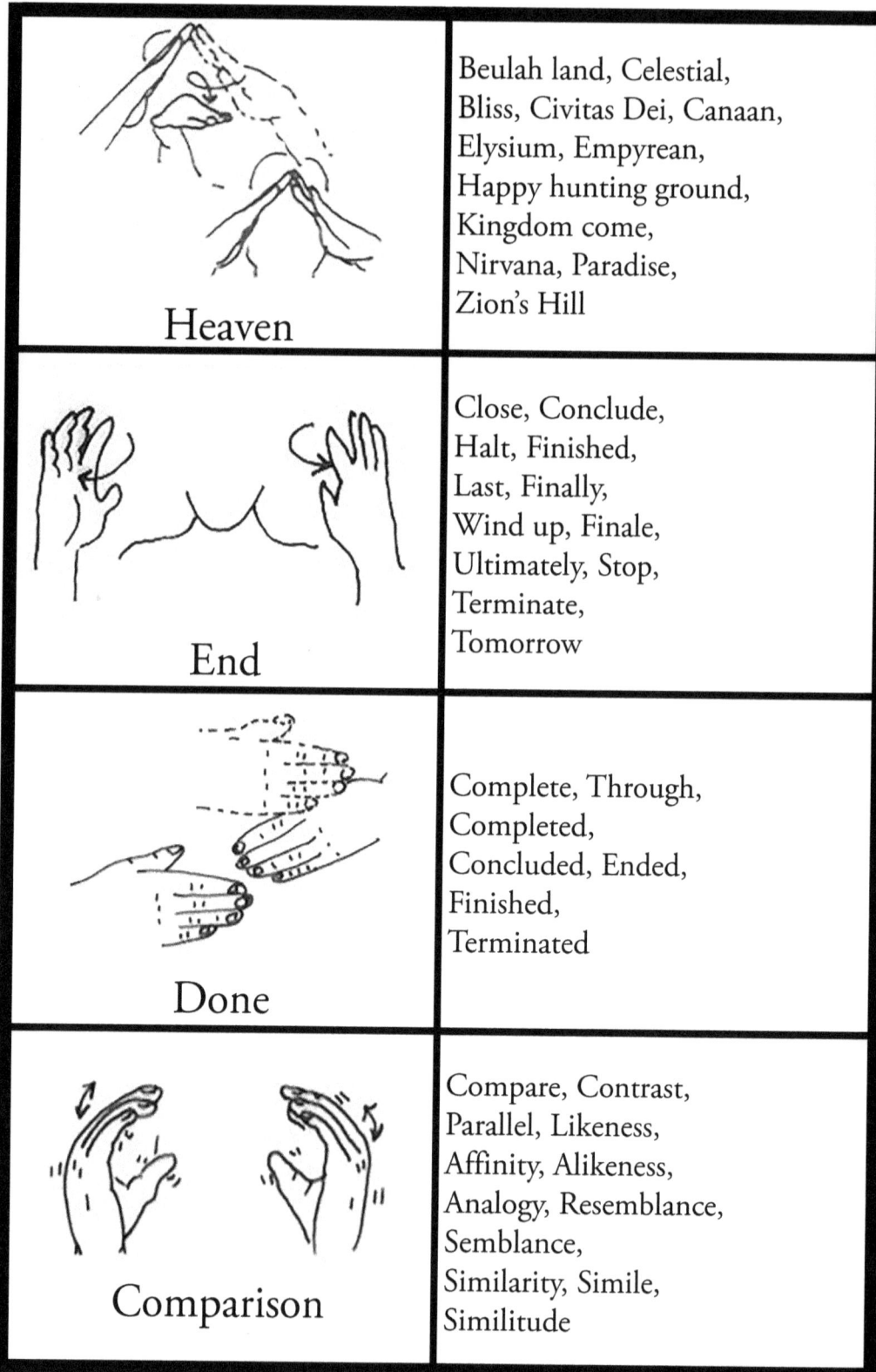

Heaven	Beulah land, Celestial, Bliss, Civitas Dei, Canaan, Elysium, Empyrean, Happy hunting ground, Kingdom come, Nirvana, Paradise, Zion's Hill
End	Close, Conclude, Halt, Finished, Last, Finally, Wind up, Finale, Ultimately, Stop, Terminate, Tomorrow
Done	Complete, Through, Completed, Concluded, Ended, Finished, Terminated
Comparison	Compare, Contrast, Parallel, Likeness, Affinity, Alikeness, Analogy, Resemblance, Semblance, Similarity, Simile, Similitude

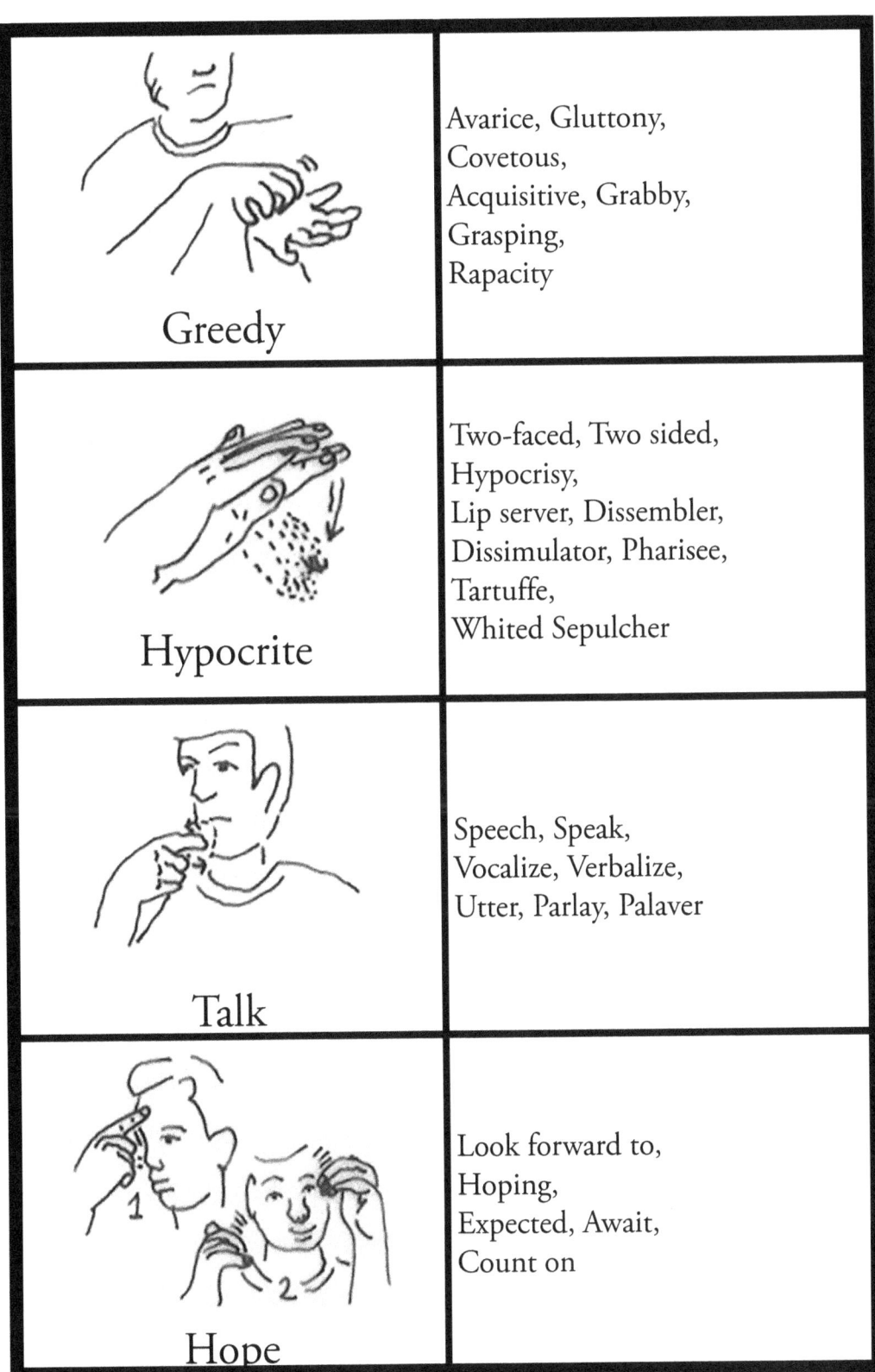

Greedy	Avarice, Gluttony, Covetous, Acquisitive, Grabby, Grasping, Rapacity
Hypocrite	Two-faced, Two sided, Hypocrisy, Lip server, Dissembler, Dissimulator, Pharisee, Tartuffe, Whited Sepulcher
Talk	Speech, Speak, Vocalize, Verbalize, Utter, Parlay, Palaver
Hope	Look forward to, Hoping, Expected, Await, Count on

Before (in front of)	Face to face, Confront
Introduce	Present, Acquaint
Meet	Met, Meeting, Encounter
Care	Caring Keep, Oversee, Charge, Supervise, Concern, Heed, Careful, Regard, Custody, Guardianship, Ward, Safekeeping, Provide

Limit	Confines, Bounds, Boundary, Term, Limitation, Restrict
Eager	Desirous, Earnest, Intent, Over anxious, Agog, Anxious, Appetent, Ardent, Athirst, Avid, Breathless, Impatient, Keen, Raring, Solicitous
Nervous	Anxiety, Jittery, Jumpy, Nervousness, Fidgety, Goosey, High-strung, Nervy, Un-restful
Heavenly Father	Great Father

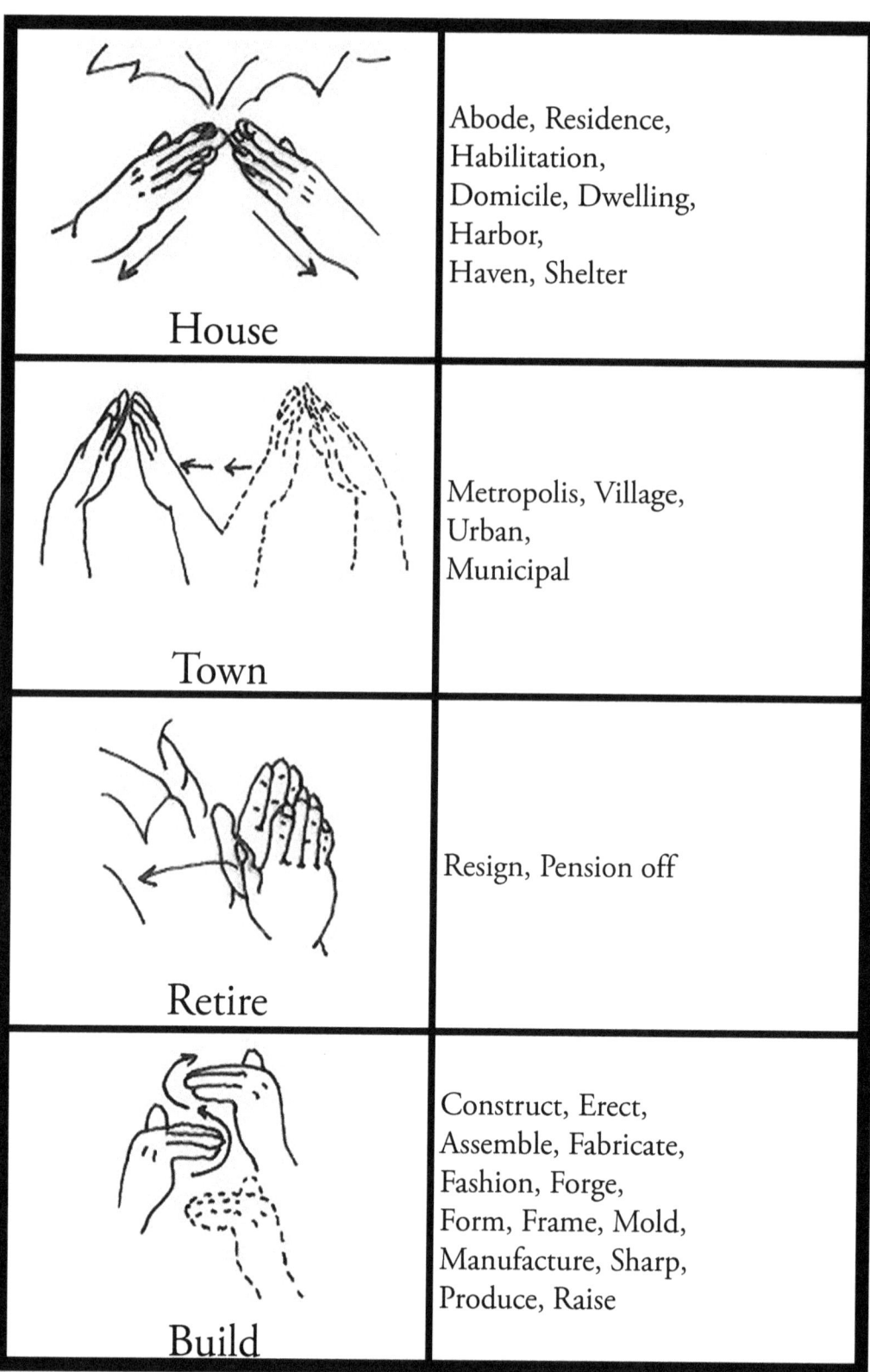

House	Abode, Residence, Habilitation, Domicile, Dwelling, Harbor, Haven, Shelter
Town	Metropolis, Village, Urban, Municipal
Retire	Resign, Pension off
Build	Construct, Erect, Assemble, Fabricate, Fashion, Forge, Form, Frame, Mold, Manufacture, Sharp, Produce, Raise

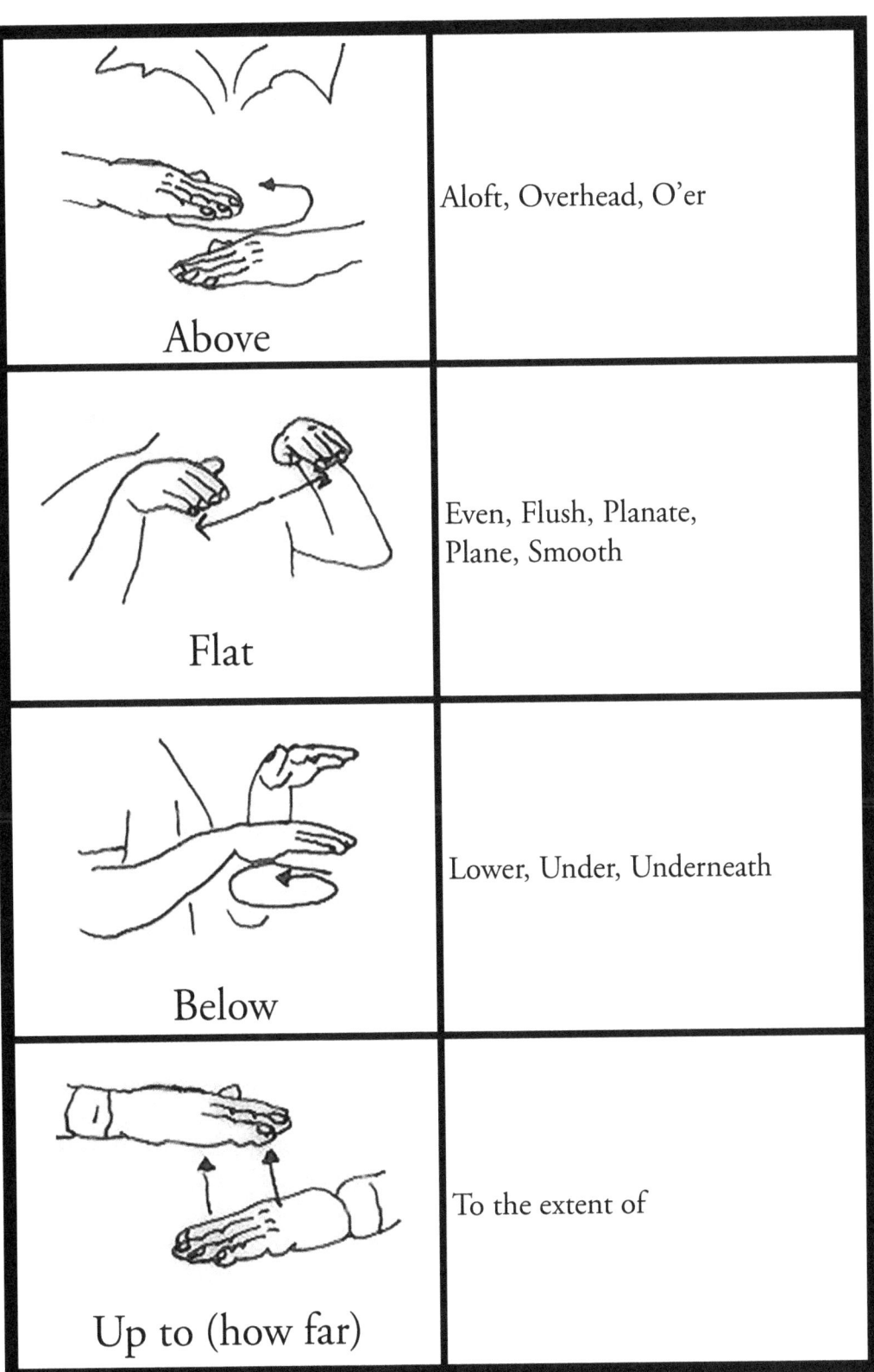

Above	Aloft, Overhead, O'er
Flat	Even, Flush, Planate, Plane, Smooth
Below	Lower, Under, Underneath
Up to (how far)	To the extent of

Share	Ration, Portion, A lot, Cut, Allotment, Allowance, Apportionment, Quantum
Divide	Distribute, Dichotomize, Split up, Part
After	Beyond, Afterward, Subsequently, Following, Ensuing
Before (time span)	Beforehand, Pre, Previously, Ahead of, Ere, Preceding, Prior to

 Divorce	Annulment
 Separate	Detach, Disconnect, Divide, Part, Dichotomize, Disjoin, Disjoint, Dissect, Disunite, Rupture, Sever, Split up, Sunder, Un-combine
 Peace	Harmony, Tranquility
 Bed	Cot, Bunk

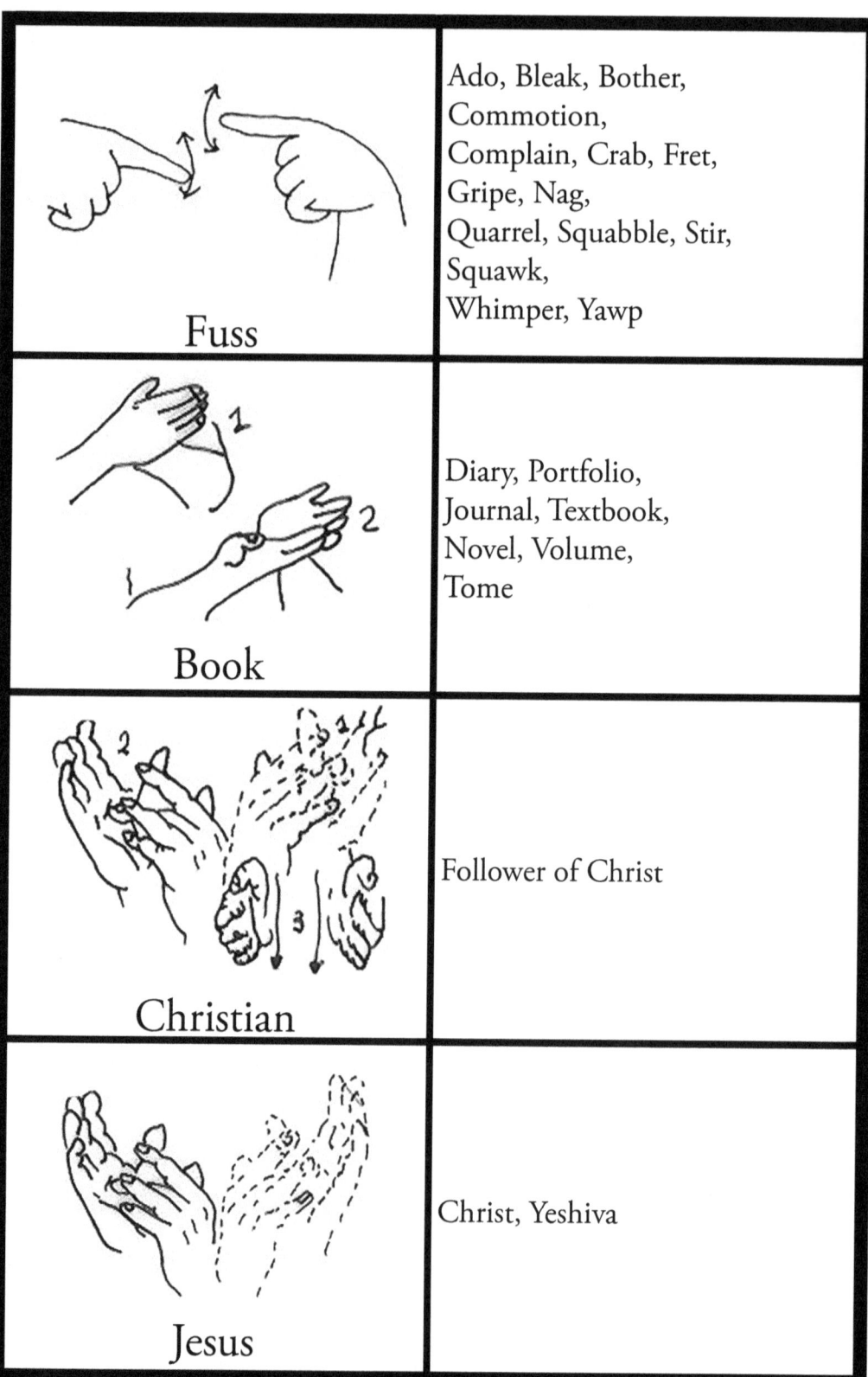

Fuss	Ado, Bleak, Bother, Commotion, Complain, Crab, Fret, Gripe, Nag, Quarrel, Squabble, Stir, Squawk, Whimper, Yawp
Book	Diary, Portfolio, Journal, Textbook, Novel, Volume, Tome
Christian	Follower of Christ
Jesus	Christ, Yeshiva

Debate	Agitate, Differ, Argumentation Argue, Discuss, Moot, Pro and Con, Trash out, Toss around
Answer	Come back, Come in, Rejoinder, Reply, Respond, Response, Result, Report
Speak	Articulate, Converse, Say, Talk, Utter, Verbalize, Vocalize, Voice
Knife	Blade, Cutlery

	Bow wow, Canine, Hound, Pooch, Pup, Puppy
Dog	
Pick on	Nag, Henpeck
Champion	Blue Ribbon, First place,
Word	Term

Show	Demonstrate, Display, Exhibit, Illustrate
Show off	Exhibitionist, Hot shot, Brandish, Flash, Flaunt
Example	Model, Specimen, Instance, Illustration, Sample
Hamburger	Ground meat, Patty

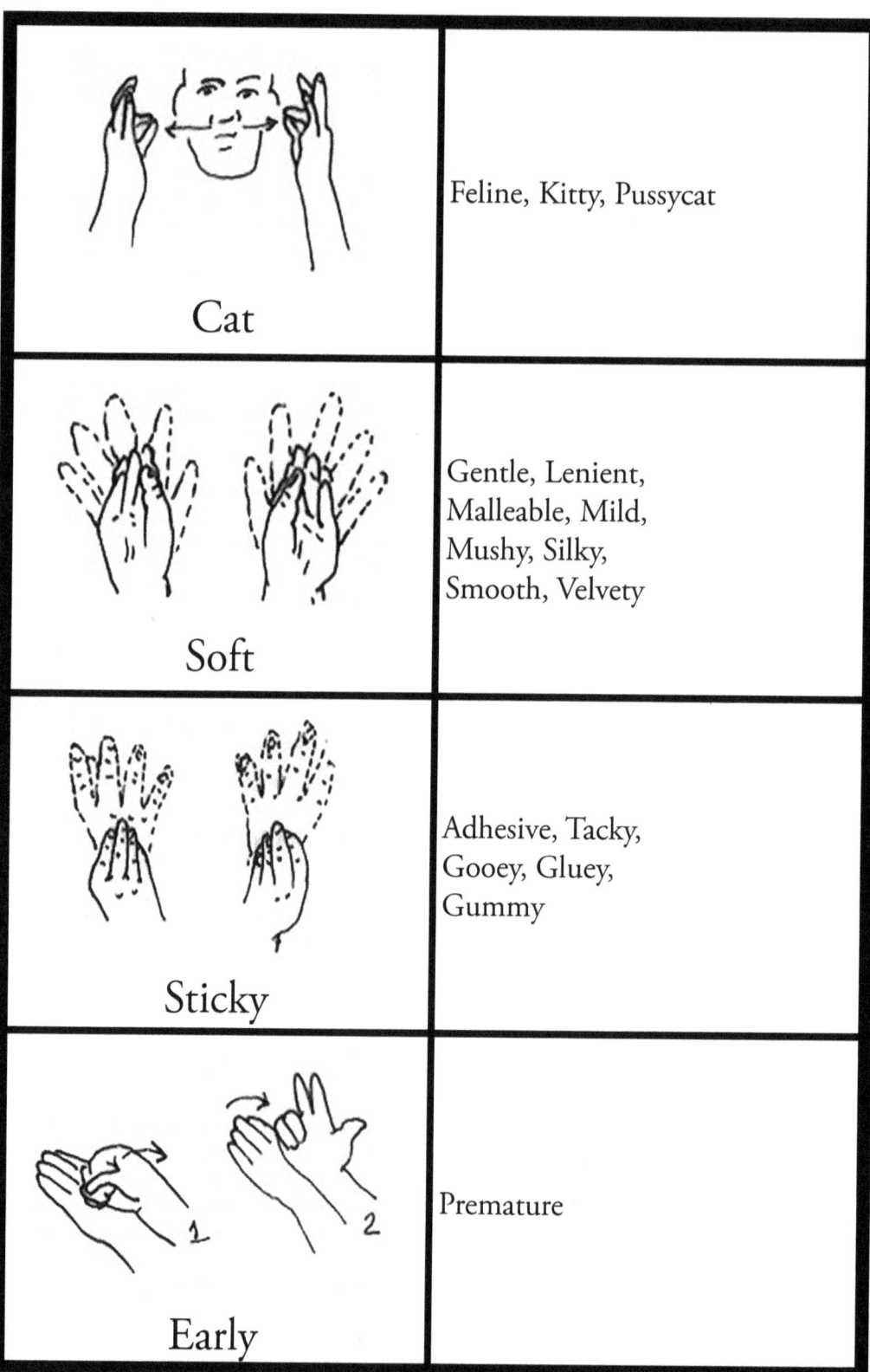

Cat	Feline, Kitty, Pussycat
Soft	Gentle, Lenient, Malleable, Mild, Mushy, Silky, Smooth, Velvety
Sticky	Adhesive, Tacky, Gooey, Gluey, Gummy
Early	Premature

Bug	Spider, Insect
War	Combat, Battle
Rain	Precipitation, Drizzle, Showers, Down pour
Disappear	Fade, Die out, Dim, Dissolve, Dull, Vanish

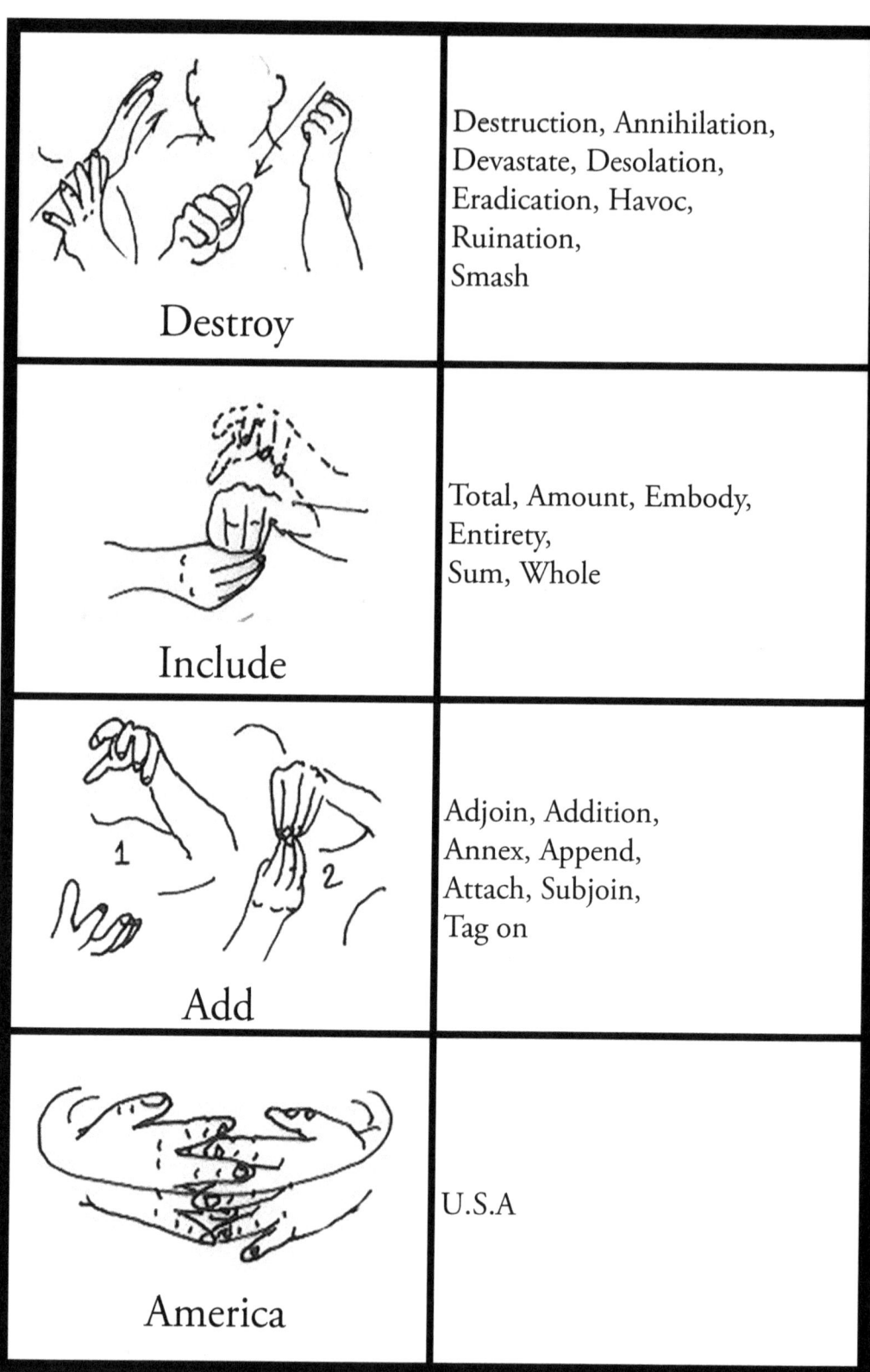

Destroy	Destruction, Annihilation, Devastate, Desolation, Eradication, Havoc, Ruination, Smash
Include	Total, Amount, Embody, Entirety, Sum, Whole
Add	Adjoin, Addition, Annex, Append, Attach, Subjoin, Tag on
America	U.S.A

Freeze	Paralyze, Petrify, Not move, Stop, Ice
Piano	Keyboard
Wait	Linger, Try
Assume	Take up

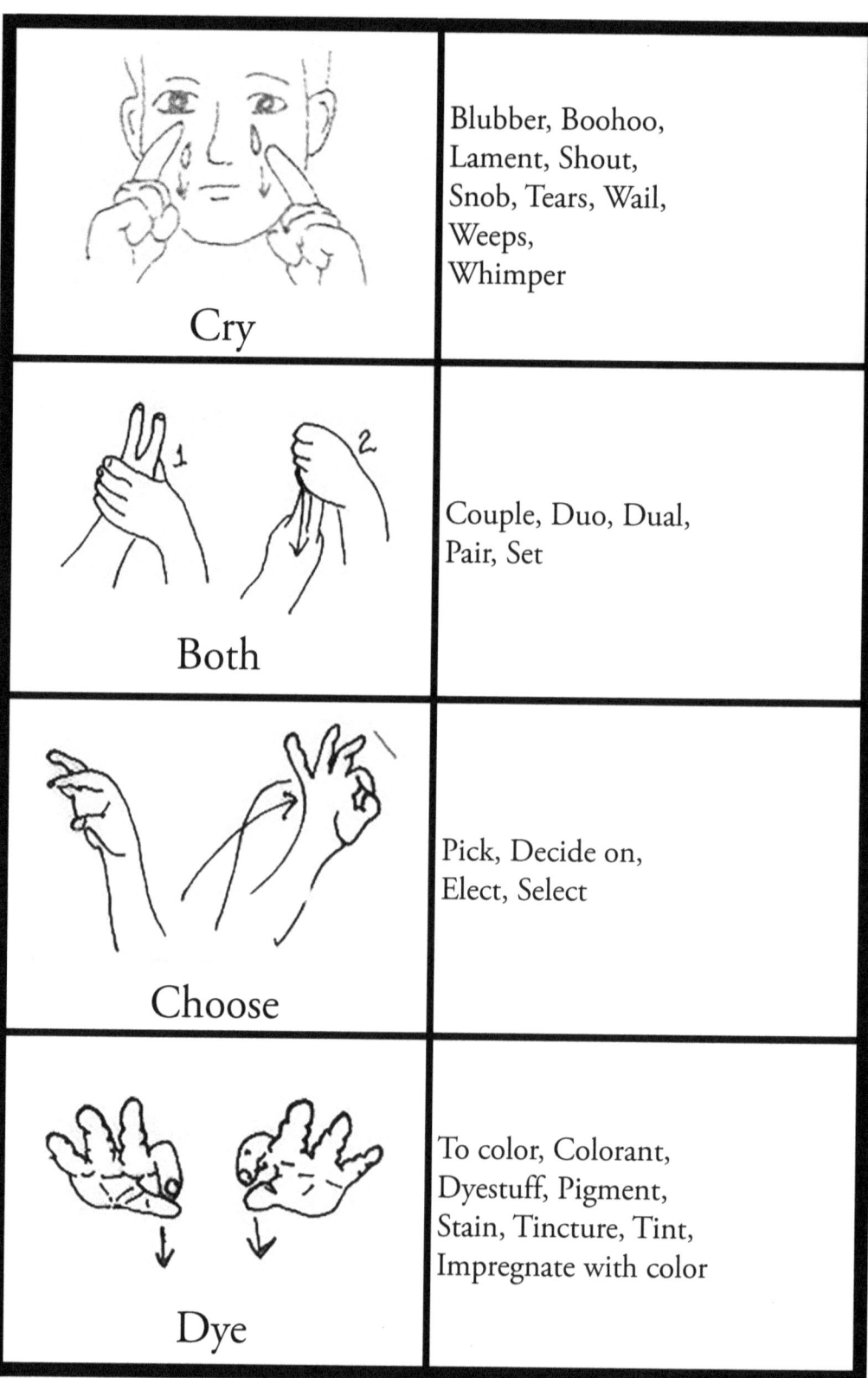

Cry	Blubber, Boohoo, Lament, Shout, Snob, Tears, Wail, Weeps, Whimper
Both	Couple, Duo, Dual, Pair, Set
Choose	Pick, Decide on, Elect, Select
Dye	To color, Colorant, Dyestuff, Pigment, Stain, Tincture, Tint, Impregnate with color

Milk	Milk a cow
Alligator	Crocodile, Caiman
Chocolate	Cocoa
Where	Everywhere, Location, In what direction?, In what place?, In which position?, Whereabouts, Wherever, Whither

Ambulance	Emergency vehicle
Dictionary	Glossary, Jargon, Lexicon, Palaver, Terminology, Vocabulary
Dollar	Bill, Buck, Legal tender, Oner
Except	All but, Aside, Apart from, But, Except for, Excluding, Exclusive of, Save

Deviat	Depart, Digress, Diverge, Off the point, Ramble, Stray, Swerve, Turn, Veer, Wander
Emergency	Catastrophe, Crisis, Exigency
Empty	Gone, Bare, Blank, Disappear, Uninhabited, Vacant, Vacuous, Vanished, Void
Play	Amusement, Disport, Diversion, Frolic, Game, Jest, Recreation, Romp

Sin	Iniquity, Transgress, Transgression, Vice, wrong doing
Agree	Accord, Accommodate, Admit, Acknowledge, Assent, Accede, Consist Acquiescence, Cohere, Coincide, In concert, Concord, Concur, Conform, Consent, t, Consort, Correspond, Dovetail, Recognize, Comport,
Socks	Woolies, Booties
Stockings	Hose, Hosiery, Nylons, Panty hose

Anchor	Catch, Fashion, Fix, Grappling iron, Moor, Secure
Shame	Contempt, Debase, Discredit, Disesteem, Disfavor, Disgrace, Dishonor, Disrepute, Embarrass, Humble, Humiliate, Mortify, Ignominy, Infamy, Obloquy, Opprobrium, Reproach
Today	At this time, This day, In the present, Now, Presently, On this day
Challenge	Confront, Duel, Competition, Brave, To dare

 Big headed	Haughty, Big shot
 Fantasize	Fantasy, Imagine, Dream, Hallucinate
 Invent	Contrive, Concoct, Cook up, Create, Design, Devise, Dream up, Formulate, Hatch up, Innovate, Make up, Originate, Vamp up
 Race	Charge, Contest, Competition, Career, Dash, Marathon

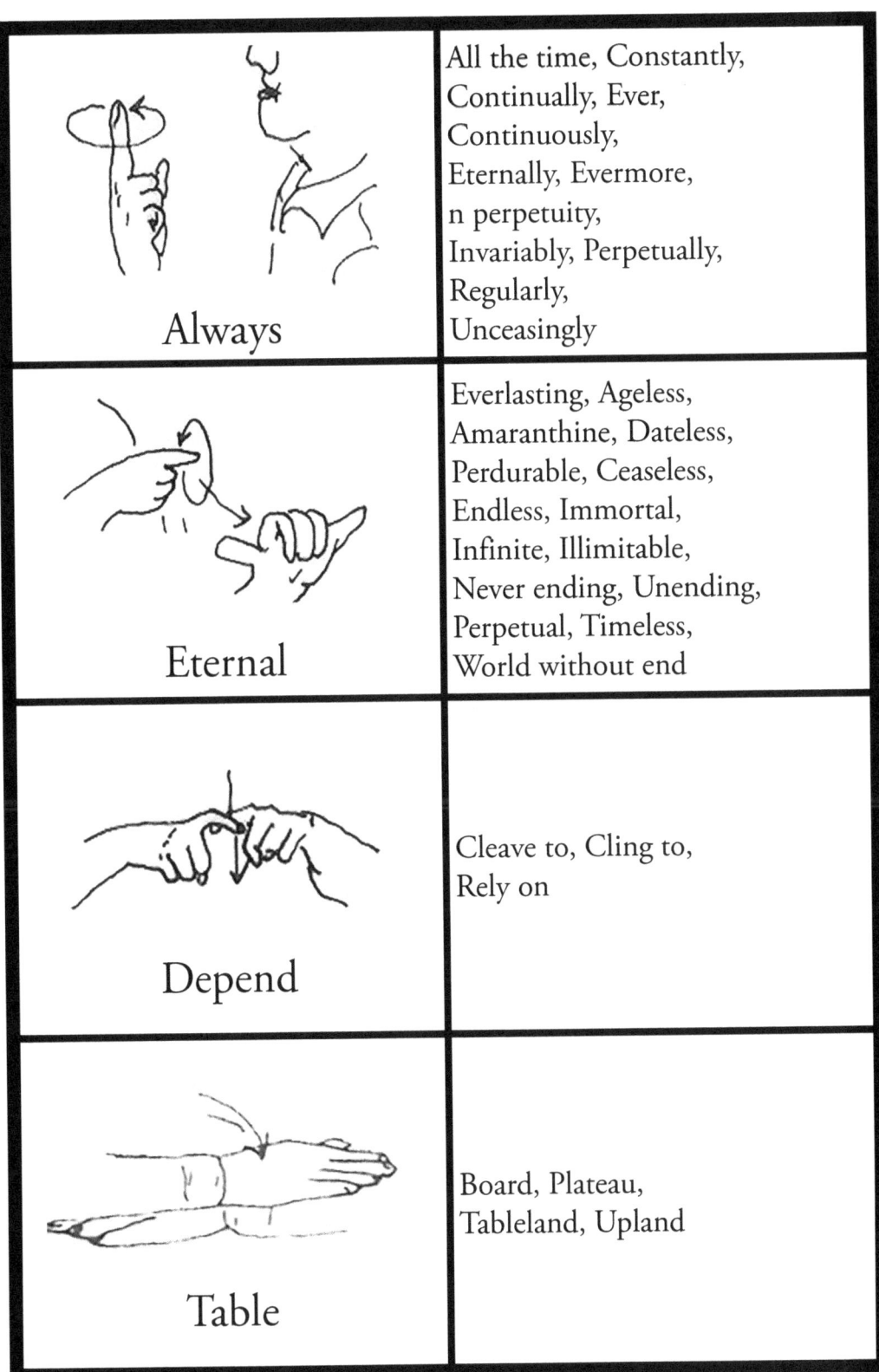

Always

All the time, Constantly, Continually, Ever, Continuously, Eternally, Evermore, n perpetuity, Invariably, Perpetually, Regularly, Unceasingly

Eternal

Everlasting, Ageless, Amaranthine, Dateless, Perdurable, Ceaseless, Endless, Immortal, Infinite, Illimitable, Never ending, Unending, Perpetual, Timeless, World without end

Depend

Cleave to, Cling to, Rely on

Table

Board, Plateau, Tableland, Upland

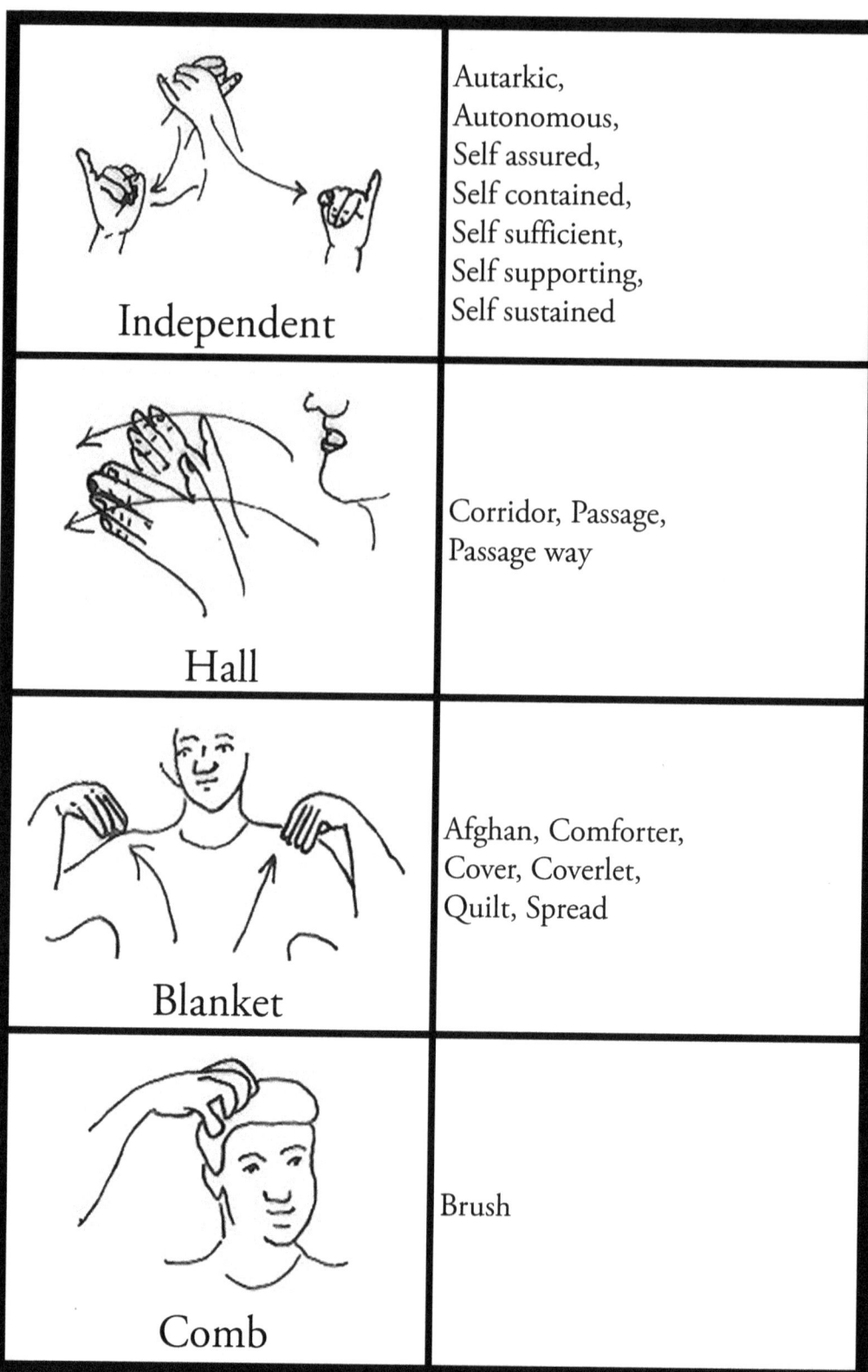

Independent	Autarkic, Autonomous, Self assured, Self contained, Self sufficient, Self supporting, Self sustained
Hall	Corridor, Passage, Passage way
Blanket	Afghan, Comforter, Cover, Coverlet, Quilt, Spread
Comb	Brush

Frustrate	Agitated, Baffled, Bilked, Buffaloed, Dashed, Disappointed, Foiled, Irritated, Thwarted
Suffer	Agonize, Bear, Endure, Tolerate
Danger	Endanger, Harmful, Hazard, Jeopardy, Peril, -ious, Risk, -y, Parlous, Treacherous, Chancy
Same	Like, As, Also, Too, Alike, Exact, Additionally, Common, Consistent, Constant, Duplicate, Equal, Identical, Equivalent, Indistinguishable, Invariable, Selfsame, Similar, Standard, Such, Unchanging, Unfailing

Push	Compress, Drive, Nudge, Press, Pressure, Propel, Shove, Thrust
Pull	Drag, Draw, Extract, Haul, Jug, Tear, Tug, Tow, Yank
Same	Alike, Consistent, Constant, Duplicate, Equal, Equivalent, Identical, Similar, Indistinguishable, Like, Unchanging, Unfailing
Oh Yes I See	I get it, I understand, Is that so?

Down	Below, Downward
Up	Arise, Ascend, Aspire
Wrestle	Brawl, Grapple, Scuffle, Struggle, Tangle, Tussle
Computer	Data processor

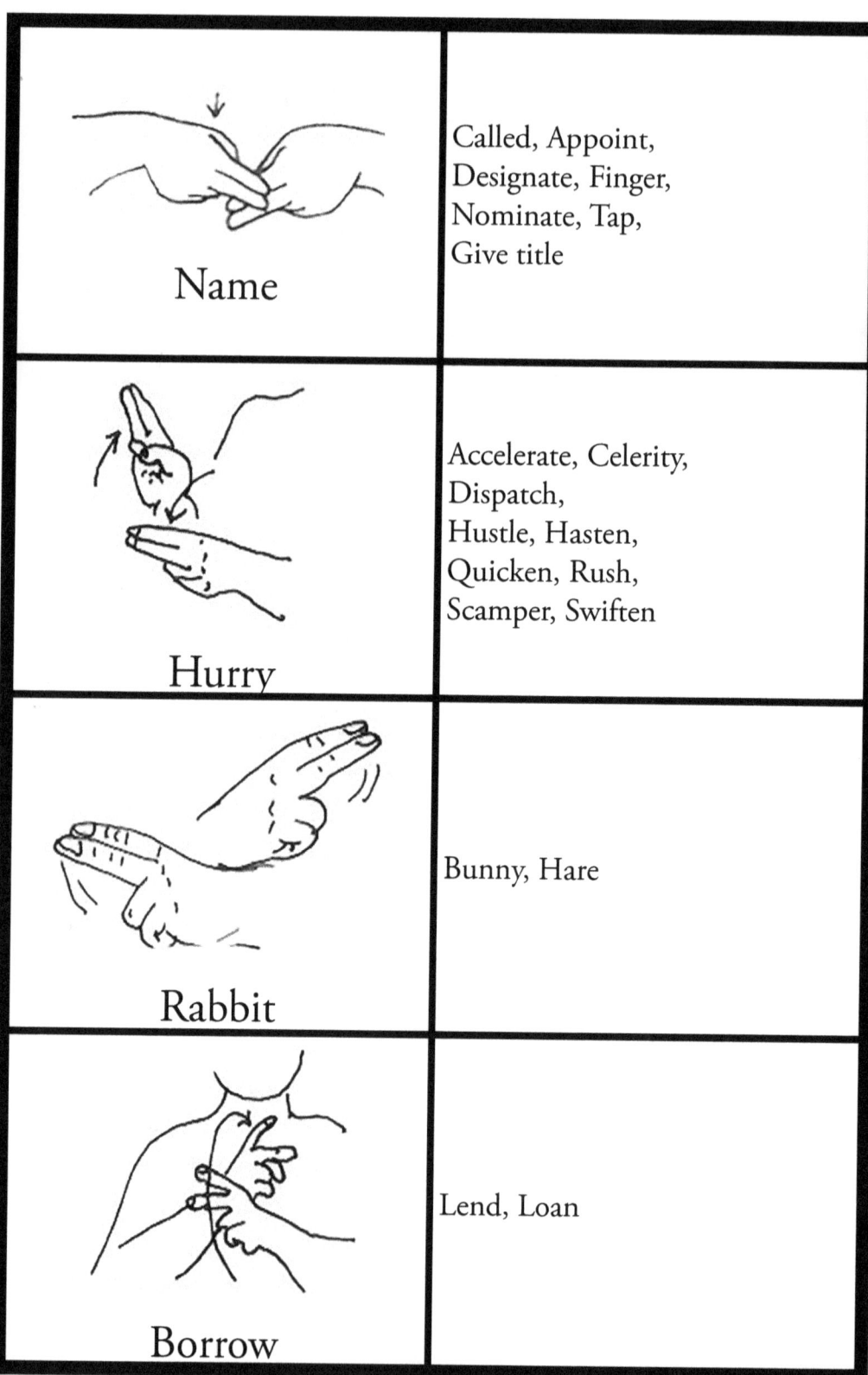

Name	Called, Appoint, Designate, Finger, Nominate, Tap, Give title
Hurry	Accelerate, Celerity, Dispatch, Hustle, Hasten, Quicken, Rush, Scamper, Swiften
Rabbit	Bunny, Hare
Borrow	Lend, Loan

Supervise	Monitor, Patrol, Take care of, Oversee, Chaperon, Overlook, Superintend
Plate	Platter
Rocking chair	Rocker
Give	Distribute, Hand out, Pass out, Present, Donate, Grant, Provide, Dish out, Deliver, Dispense, Furnish, Supply

Move	Relocate, Position, Place, Movement
Charge	Fee, Fare, Price, Tax, Levy, Fine, Lien, Cost, Rate, Tab, Tariff
Goodbye	Bye, So long, Farewell
Gift	Present, Award, Contribution, Donation, Reward, Tribute, Benevolence

Let	Allow, Grant, Leave, Permit, Suffer
Permission	Let, Allow, Permit, Authorize, Consent
People	Folk, Public
Kitchen	Mess Hall, Galley, Dining hall

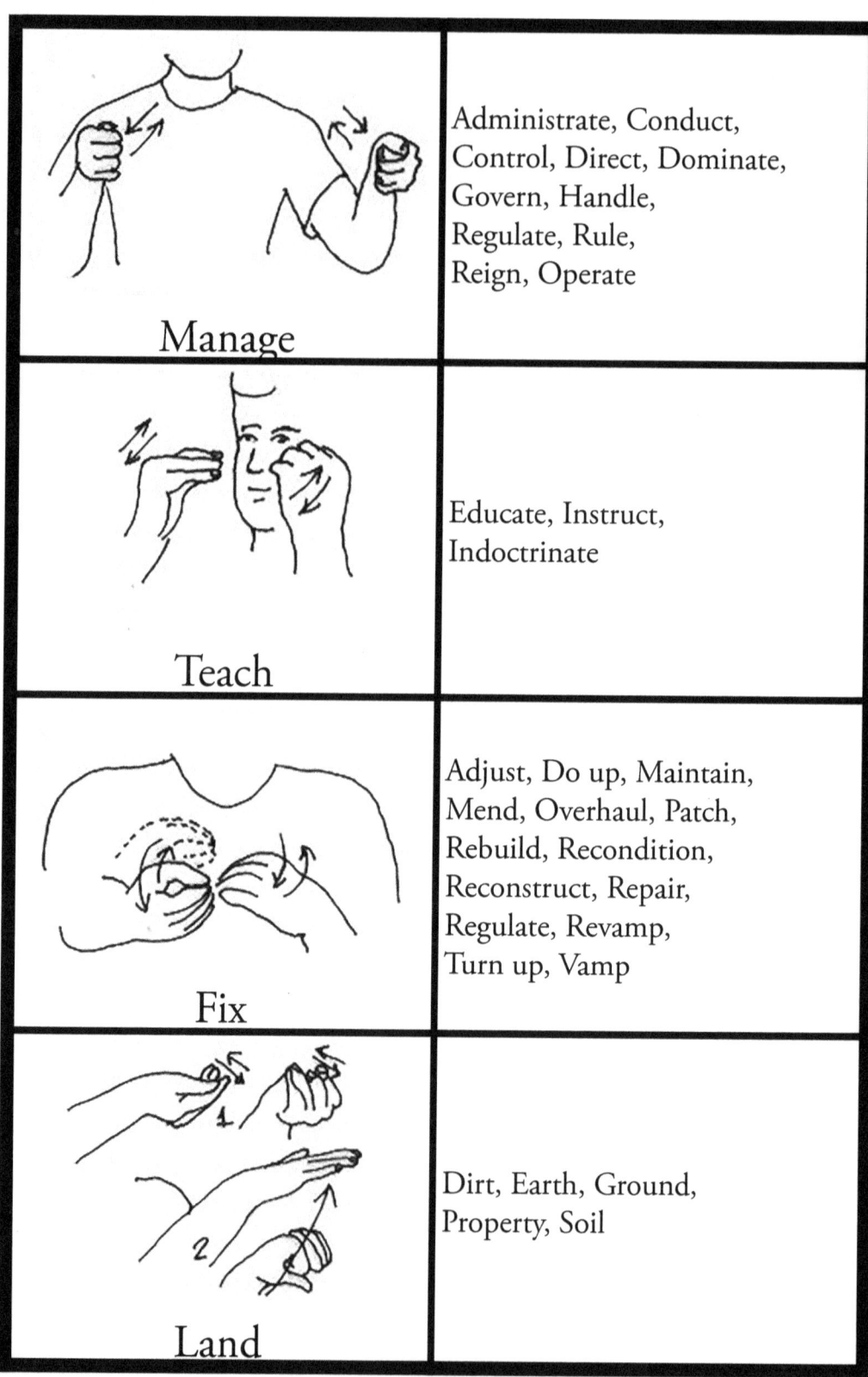

Manage	Administrate, Conduct, Control, Direct, Dominate, Govern, Handle, Regulate, Rule, Reign, Operate
Teach	Educate, Instruct, Indoctrinate
Fix	Adjust, Do up, Maintain, Mend, Overhaul, Patch, Rebuild, Recondition, Reconstruct, Repair, Regulate, Revamp, Turn up, Vamp
Land	Dirt, Earth, Ground, Property, Soil

Spread(tell abroad)	Tell, Declare, Proclaim, Announce, Advertise
Gossip	Blab, Carry tale, Circulator, Gad, Mumble news, Rumor, Rumor monger, Scandalize, Tale bearer, Buzz, Grapevine, Hearsay
Restroom	Toilet, Men's/Ladies room, Lavatory, Washroom, Powder room
Toilet	Commode, Convenience, Head, John, Privy, Johnny, Latrine, Lavatory, Restroom, Water closet

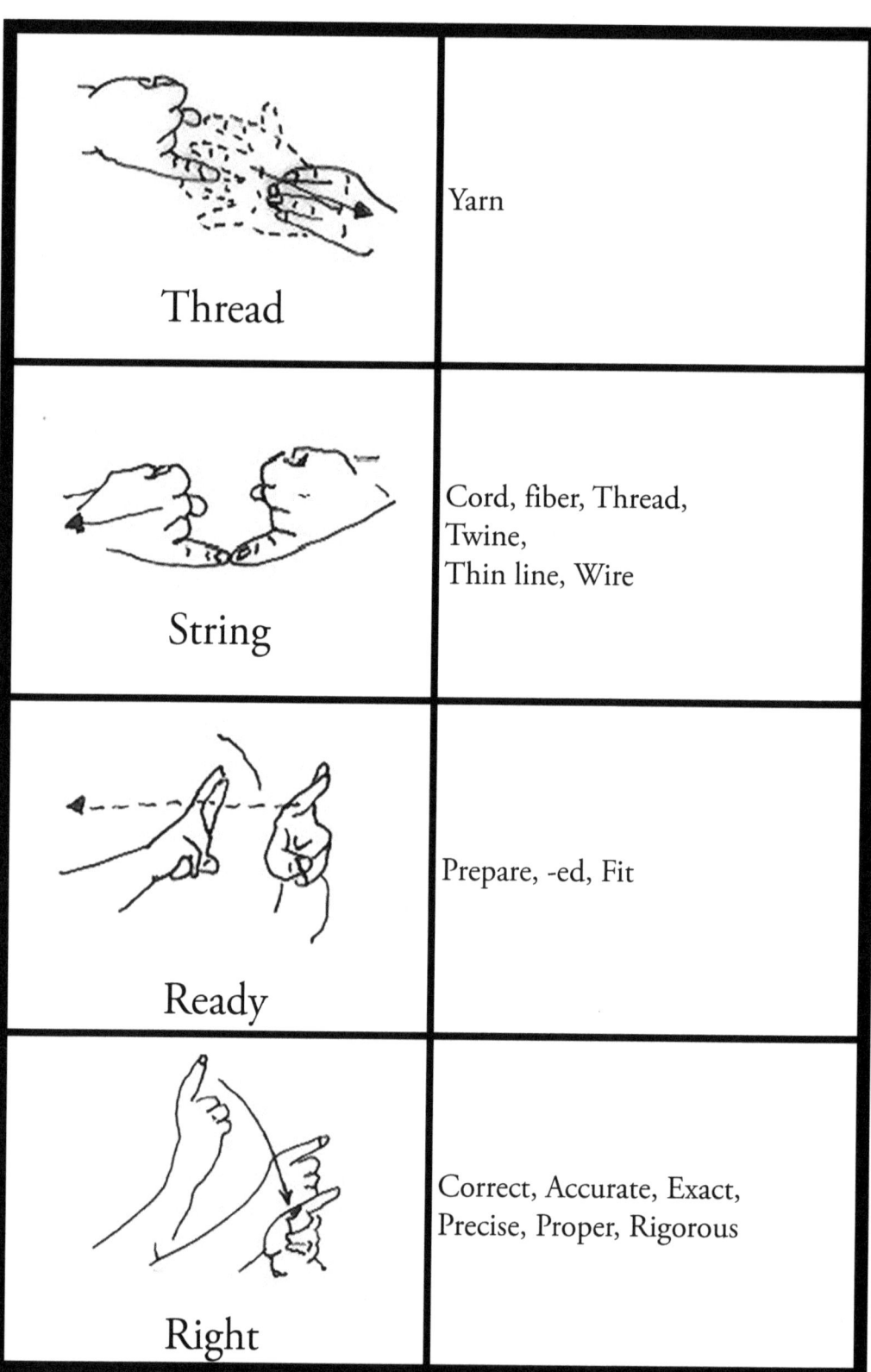

Thread	Yarn
String	Cord, fiber, Thread, Twine, Thin line, Wire
Ready	Prepare, -ed, Fit
Right	Correct, Accurate, Exact, Precise, Proper, Rigorous

Spread	Circulate, -ed, Diffuse, Dispersed, Disseminate, Distribute, Epidemic, Expand, Extend, Fan out, Outspread, Outstretch, Propagate, Strew, Unfold
Clear	Clarify, Bright, Clarion, Fair, Cloudless, Evident, Fine, Glitter, Glisten, Pellucid, Illuminate, Light, Limpid, Rainless, Shine, Sunny, Lucid Radiant, Translucent, Lucent Transparent, Unclouded, Beaming, Brilliant, Effulgent, Fulgent, Incandescent,
Store	Market, Mart, Outlet, Shop, Showroom
Sell	Market, Merchandise, Peddle, Retail, Vend

Last	Closing, Concluding, End, Final, Finally, Hindmost, Rearmost, Terminal, Ultimate
Boss	Authority, Chaperon, Chief, Head, Chieftain, Commander, Dominator, Headman, Honcho, Manager, Master, Overlook, Overseer, Quarter back, Superior, Supervise, Supervisor, Superintendent
Self	Yourself, Myself, Himself, Herself
Other	Another, Else, Different, Disparate, Dissimilar, Divergent, Diverse, Otherwise

Can	Capable, May, Able
Can't	Incapable, Unable, Not permitted
Do	Execute, Act
Stay	Abide, Adjourn, Arrest, Bide, Check, Defer, Delay, Fixed, Hold off, Hold over, Hold up, Interrupt, Layover, Linger, remain

	Govern, Reign, Administrate, Preside
Rule	
	Little bit, Minute, Microscopic, Diminutive, Itsy-bitsy, Miniature, Pint size, Teensy
Tiny	
	Need, Should, Ought, Obligated, Bound, Necessary
Must	
	U.S.A., America
United States	

Her	Present
Few	Handful, Infrequent, Scarce, Scant, Rare, Scattering, Smatter, Spatter, Sprinkling
Spell	Fingerspell
Yes	Assent, Accede, All right, Aye, Consent, Exactly, OK, Okay, Precise, Subscribe, Sure, Yea

Win	Celebrate, Victory, Jubilee, Triumph, Festival, Conquest, Success, Rejoice, Conquer, Prevail, Overcome
Tie	Neckpiece
Exact	Accurate, Precise, Correct
Perfect	Flawless, Infallible, Impeccable, Faultless, Ideal, Absolute, Fleckless, Indefectible, Unflawed, Model, Unblemished, Unmarred

	Still, Persist, maintain, Endure, Abiding, Lasting
Continue	
Measure	Gauge, Scale, Size, Dimensions, Magnitude, Proportion
Hate	Despise, Loathe, Abhor, Spite, Malice, Abominate, Aversion, Detest, Disdain, Execrate
Try	Attempt, Undertake, Endeavor, Strive

189

	Reflection, Looking glass, Imager
Mirror	
	Crackpot, Crazy, Kook, Loon, Ding-a-ling, Harebrain, Screwball
Nut(person)	
	Administration, Regime
Government	
	Compassion, Pity, Leniency, Charity, Clemency, Lenity
Mercy	

Airplane	Soar, Fly, Aviate
Enemy	Adversary, Foe, Opponent, Opposition, Oppose
Friend	Neighbor, Partner, Buddy, Pal, Acquaintance, Amigo, Confidant
Electricity	Electric

Dark	Darkness, Blackness, Gloom, Dim, Dusk, Nightfall, Murky, Obscure, Somber, Renebrous
Helicopter	Chopper, Copter, Whirlybird
Attention	Focus, Concentrate, Alert, Watchful, Pay attention, Cognizant, Heed, Mark, Note, Regard
Sleep	Sleepy, Slumber, Tired, Drowsy, Nap, Exhausted, Doze, Snooze, Sluggish, Shuteye, Lethargic

Lion	King of the Jungle, King of Beasts
Noise	Clamor, Sound, blare, Racket
Disgusted	Overwrought, Fed up, Had enough, Discontented, Aggravated, Dissatisfied
Blush	Redden, Embarrassed, Flush, Glow

Goat	Billy goat, Nanny, Kid
Stupid	Ignorant, Dumb, Dunce, Blockhead, Chump, Dimwit, Dense, Dodo, Goof, Idiot, Numskull, Thick, -headed, Pinhead
Dumb	Ignorant, Dense, Moron, Dunce, Blockhead, Bonehead, Dimwit, Idiot, Numskull, Thickheaded, Pinhead
Bible	Scriptures, Good book, Jesus' Book, Holy Bile, Holy Writ, God's Word, The Canon, "The book"

Mad	Cross, Violent, Irritated, Cranky, Ticked off, Crabby, Provoked, Grumpy, Rabid, Ire, Irate, Aggravated, Furious, Enraged, Wrathful
Sad	Ejected, Sorrowful, Gloomy, Melancholy, Cast down, Unhappy, Remorse, Dismal, Mournful, Heavyhearted
Beautiful	Beauteous, Gorgeous, Ravishing, Exquisite, Awesome, Handsome, Divine
Pretty	Beautiful, Lovely, Fair, Gorgeous, Attractive, Good looking, Ravishing, Comely, Handsome, Pulchritudinous, Stunning, Delightful

Amen	Worship, Adore, Sealed, Affirmed, So be it, I agree
Don't believe	Unbelief, Skeptical, Doubt
Sex	Intimate, Relations, Marital relations, Intercourse, Love making
Camera	Take pictures, Photo

Wonder	Astonish, Concern
Remember	Recall, Recollect, Reminisce, Keep in mind, Retain, Bethink, Cite
Catholic	Catholicism
Italy	Italian

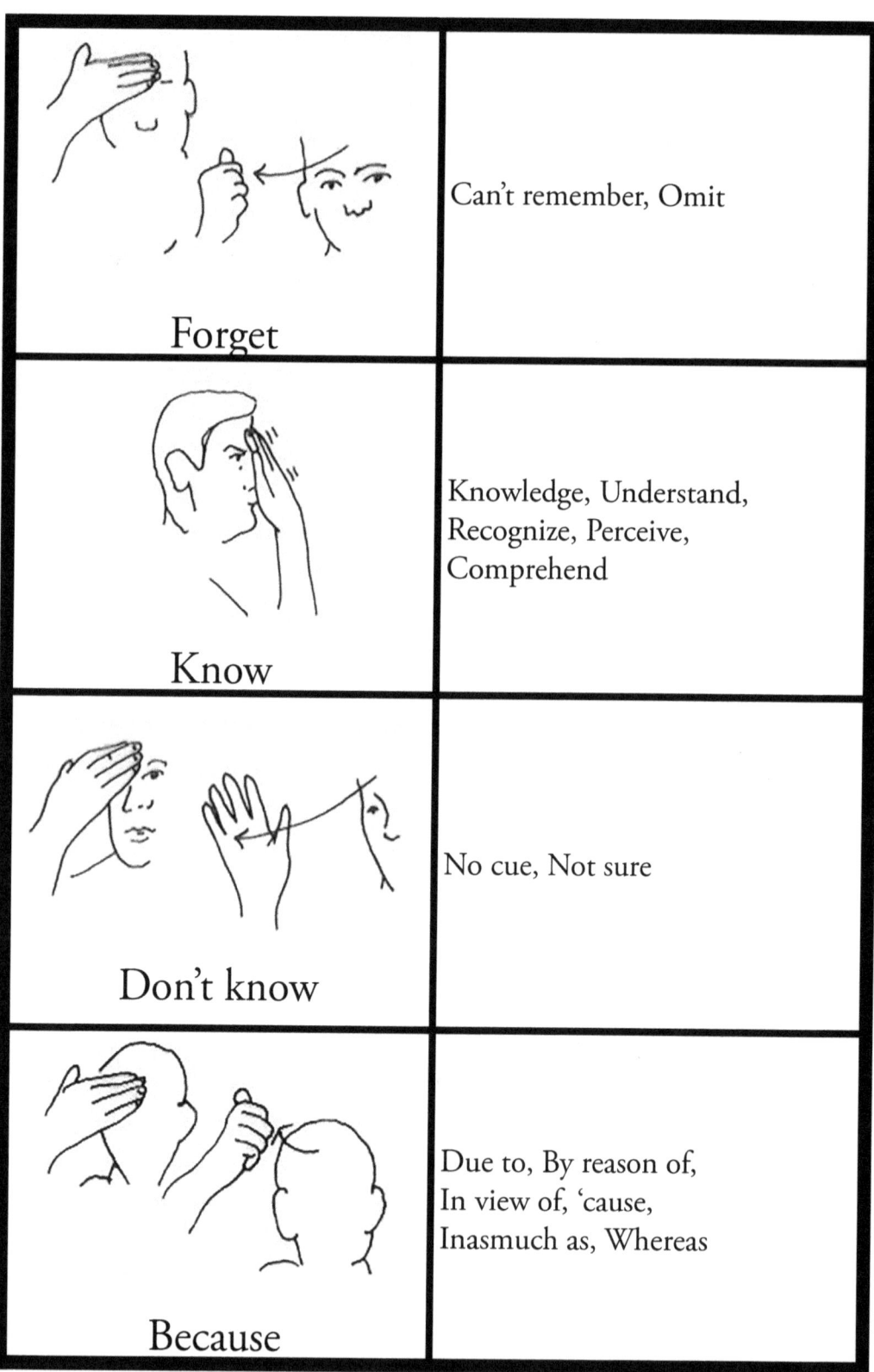

Forget	Can't remember, Omit
Know	Knowledge, Understand, Recognize, Perceive, Comprehend
Don't know	No cue, Not sure
Because	Due to, By reason of, In view of, 'cause, Inasmuch as, Whereas

Surprised	Wake up, Amazed, Awake, Aroused, Shocked, Stir, Prod, Rouse, Waken
Face	Look, Countenance, Appearance
Color	Hue, Tint, Shade, Tone, Tinge, Pigment, Cast
Why	What reason, How come, How so

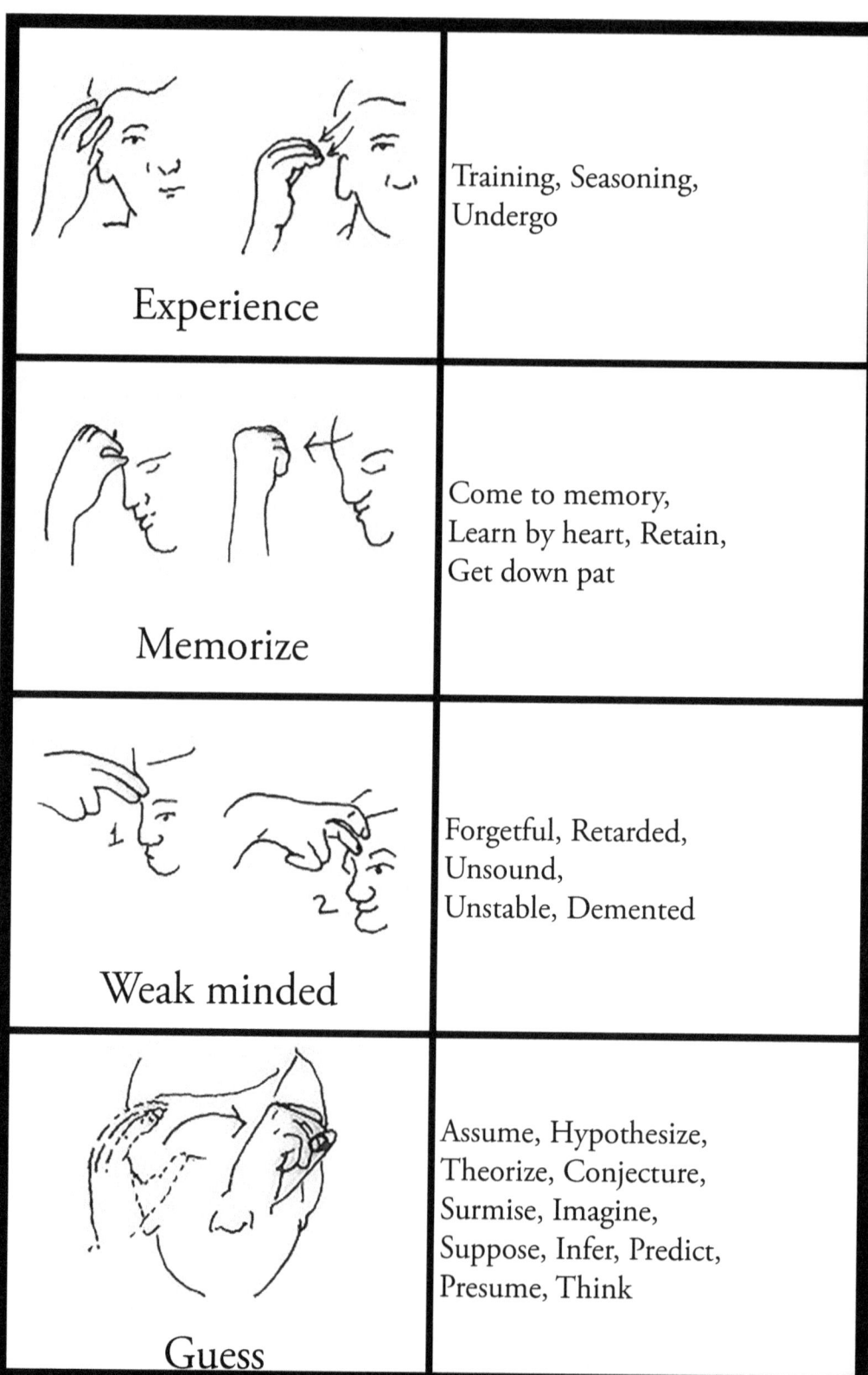

Experience	Training, Seasoning, Undergo
Memorize	Come to memory, Learn by heart, Retain, Get down pat
Weak minded	Forgetful, Retarded, Unsound, Unstable, Demented
Guess	Assume, Hypothesize, Theorize, Conjecture, Surmise, Imagine, Suppose, Infer, Predict, Presume, Think

President	Commander in chief, Chief Exec
Africa	African
China	Chinese
Japan	Japanese

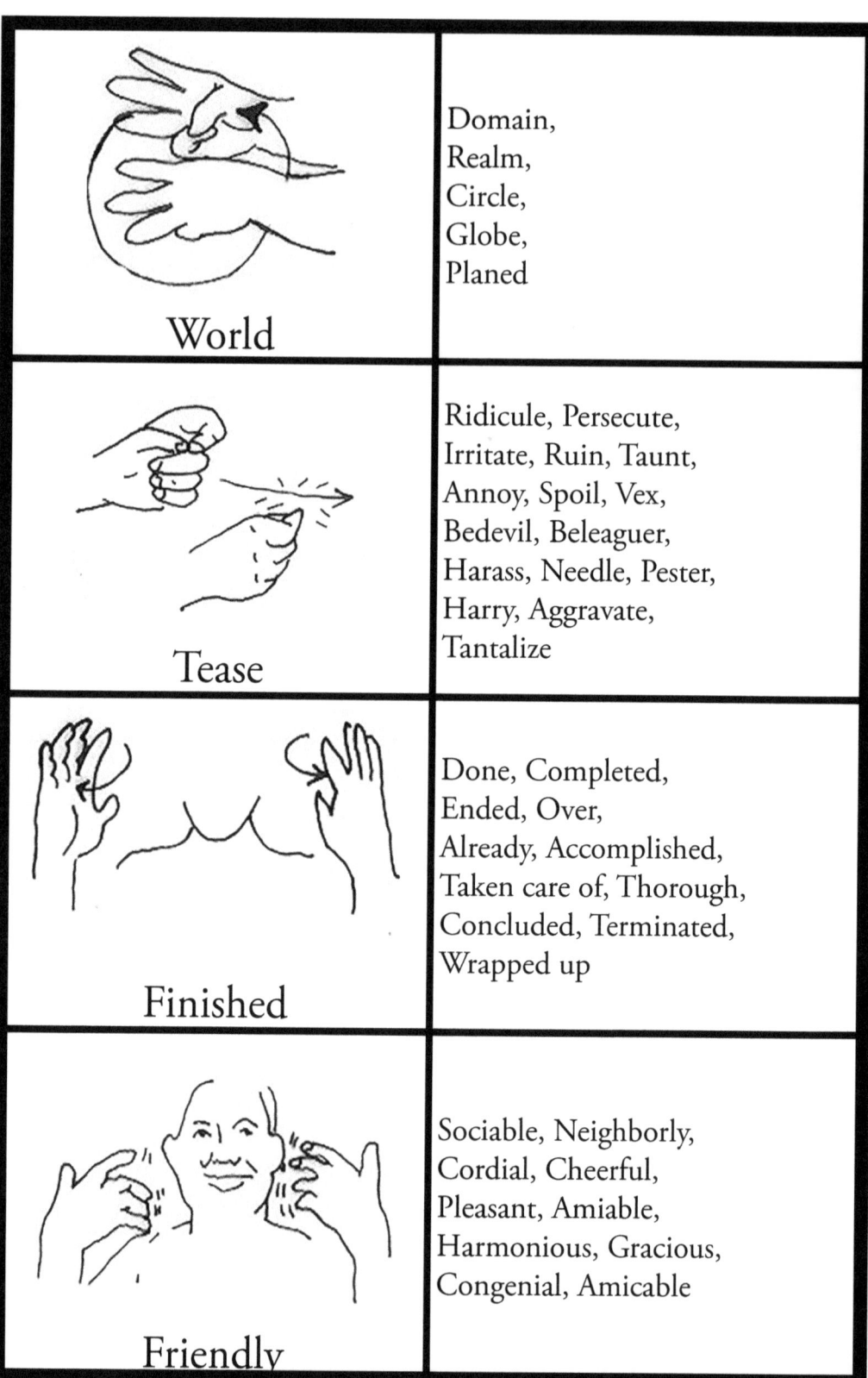

World	Domain, Realm, Circle, Globe, Planed
Tease	Ridicule, Persecute, Irritate, Ruin, Taunt, Annoy, Spoil, Vex, Bedevil, Beleaguer, Harass, Needle, Pester, Harry, Aggravate, Tantalize
Finished	Done, Completed, Ended, Over, Already, Accomplished, Taken care of, Thorough, Concluded, Terminated, Wrapped up
Friendly	Sociable, Neighborly, Cordial, Cheerful, Pleasant, Amiable, Harmonious, Gracious, Congenial, Amicable

Moon	Lunar
Notice	Observe, Heed, Note, Perceive, Recognize, Be aware of, Reveal, Detect, Regard
Radio	Boom box, Stereo, Hi fi
Crown	Tiara, Corona

  Plus	Also, Additional, Positive, Surplus, Coupled with
  Minus	Negative, Less, Subtract, Deduct
  Rent	Lease, Let, Charter, Hire
  Take away	Minus, Withdrawal, To subtract, Abort

Student	Pupil, Apprentice, Scholar, Leaner, Disciple
Hello	Hi, Greetings, Howdy, Salutations, Welcome, How
Haircut	Trim, Buzz, Ears lowered
Beauty shop	Hair Salon, Beauty Salon

Headache	Migraine
Curious	Inquisitive, Nosy, Prying, Peeping, Interested, Meddlesome, Snoopy
Egotistical	Arrogant, Conceited, Over confidant, Assuming, Prideful
Gamble	Wager, Bet, Cast lots, Stake, Game, Risk

Profit	Benefit, Gain, Advantage, Prosper, Recover, Proceeds, Return
Drug	Dope, Narcotic, Pharmaceuticals, Opiates
Between	Among, Betwixt, Amid, Within, Tween, Twix
Seal	Stamp, Authorize, Sticker, Close, Approval, Permit, Allowance

Grass	Turf, Green, Lawn, Yard
Axe	Hatchet, Hack, Whack, Chop, Cut off
Feedback	Contribute, Input, Constructive criticism
Pay	Payment, Compensate, Restitution, Wages, Refund, Salary, Award

Tape recorder	Tape player
converse	Talk, Speak to, Parley, Dialogue, Chat, Communicate, Discourse, Engage in conversation, Confabulate
Taxi	Cab
Roll	Revolve, Tumble, Turn, Turnover

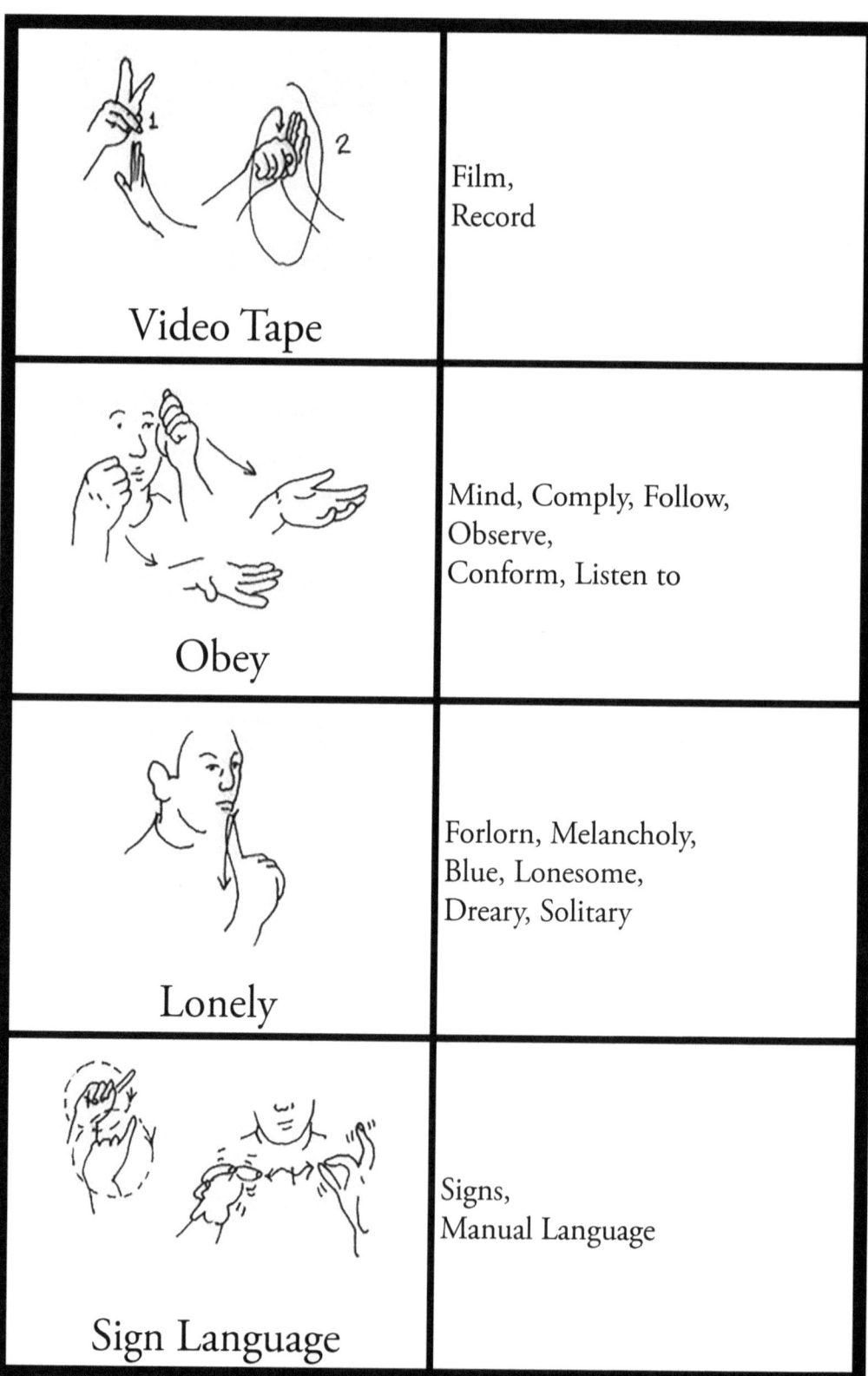

Video Tape	Film, Record
Obey	Mind, Comply, Follow, Observe, Conform, Listen to
Lonely	Forlorn, Melancholy, Blue, Lonesome, Dreary, Solitary
Sign Language	Signs, Manual Language

Forbid	Prohibit, Bar, Ban, Exclude, Inhibit, Outlaw, Taboo
Television	TV, Boob tube
Place(location)	Locate, Locality, Plot, Site, Space, Spot, Area, Territory, Point, Position, Station
Lake	Pond, Lagoon, Tarn

Multitude	Crowd, Army, Gathering, Mob, Legion, Flock, Scores, Drove, Horde, Abundance
Bless	Favor
Preach	Evangelize, Proclaim, Sermonize, Teach, Lecture
Grief	Sorrow, Anguish Bereavement, Distress, Depression, Vexation, Woe, Torment, Heartache, Crushed, Affliction, Rud

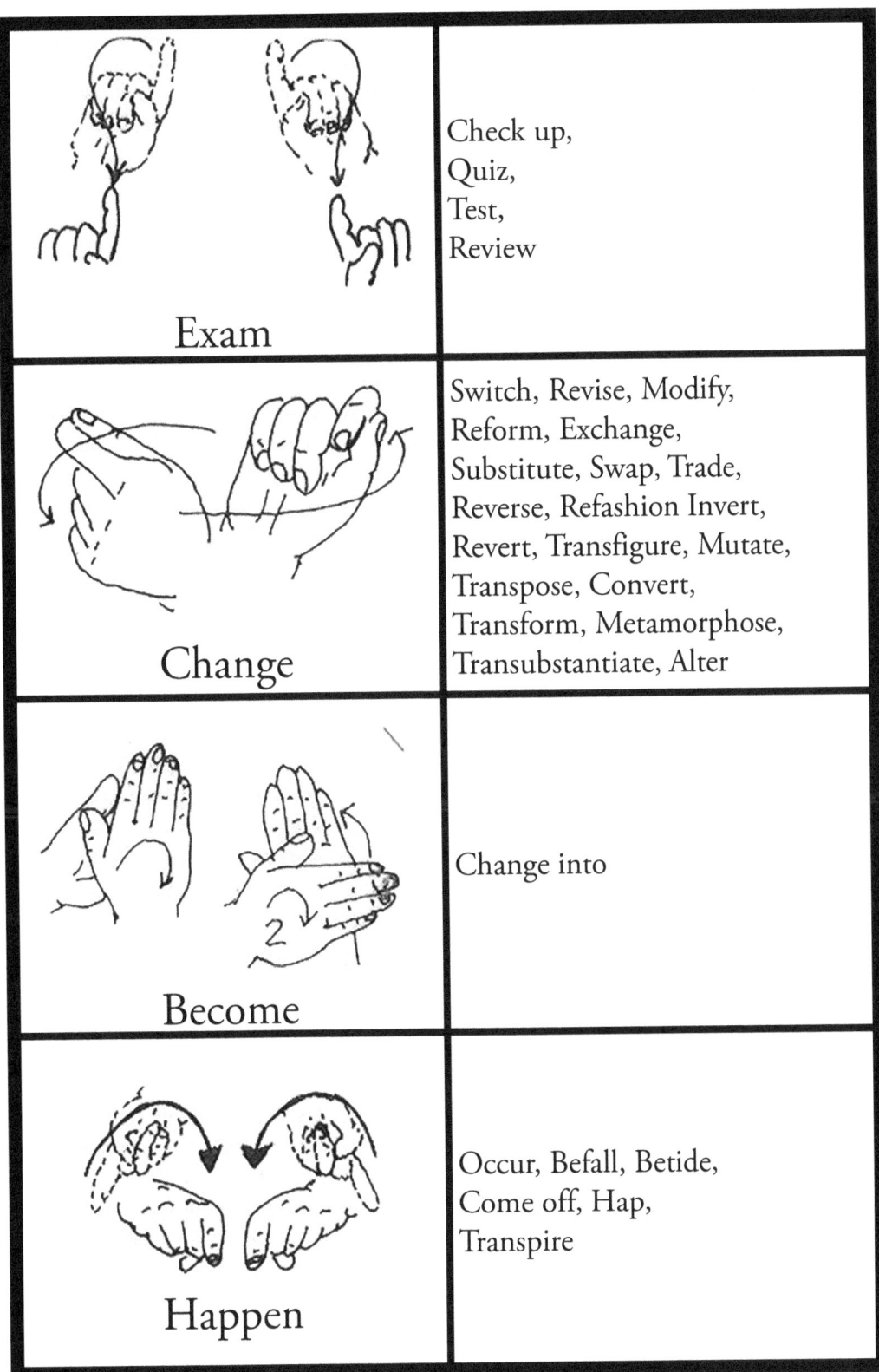

Exam	Check up, Quiz, Test, Review
Change	Switch, Revise, Modify, Reform, Exchange, Substitute, Swap, Trade, Reverse, Refashion Invert, Revert, Transfigure, Mutate, Transpose, Convert, Transform, Metamorphose, Transubstantiate, Alter
Become	Change into
Happen	Occur, Befall, Betide, Come off, Hap, Transpire

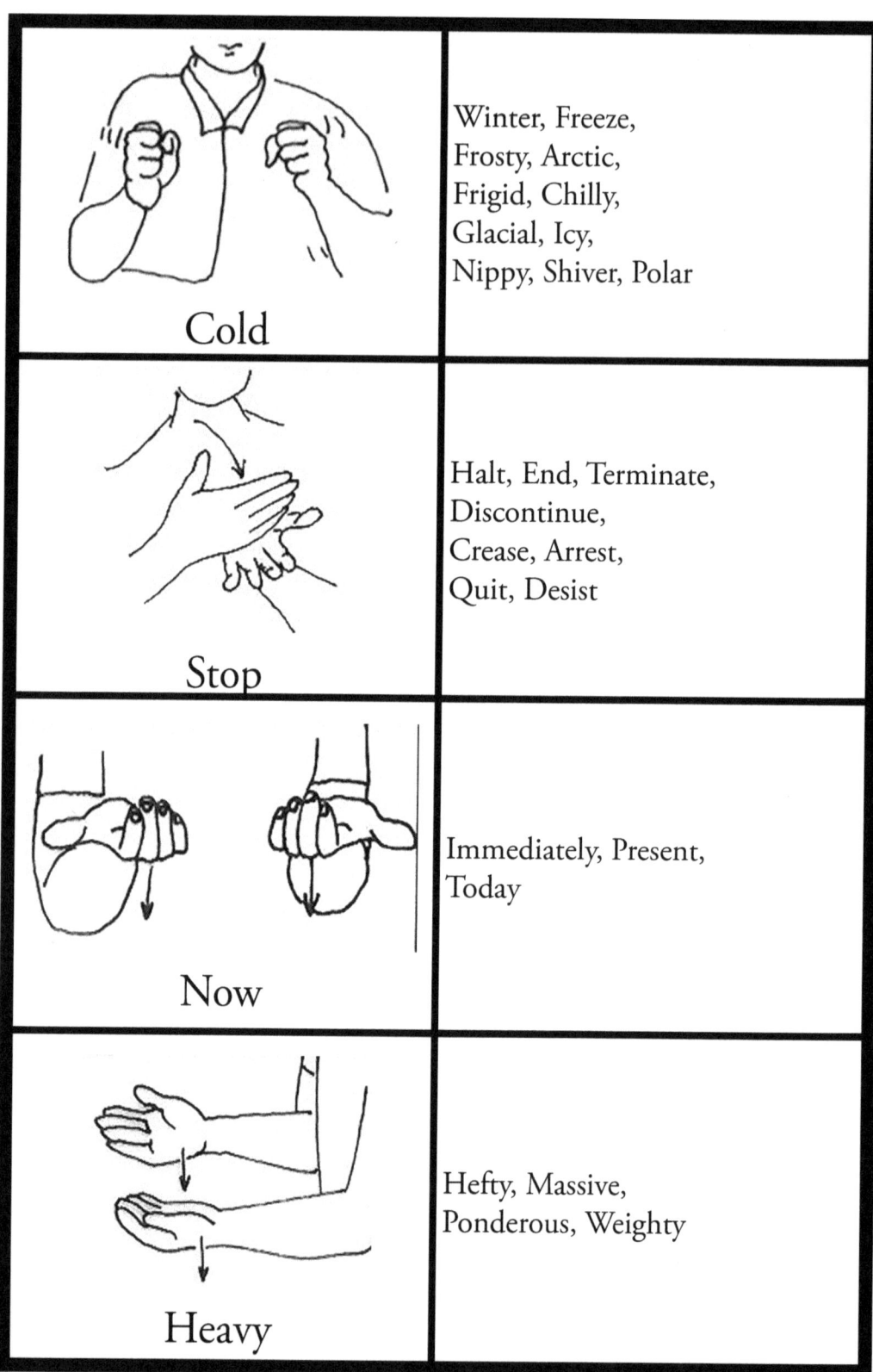

Cold	Winter, Freeze, Frosty, Arctic, Frigid, Chilly, Glacial, Icy, Nippy, Shiver, Polar
Stop	Halt, End, Terminate, Discontinue, Crease, Arrest, Quit, Desist
Now	Immediately, Present, Today
Heavy	Hefty, Massive, Ponderous, Weighty

Meeting	Assembly, Conference, Rally, Gathering, Convention, Council, Powwow, Concourse
Percent	Percentage, Portion, Interest, Radio, Quota, Share, Allotment
Rest	Relax, Lie down, Recuperate, Ease, Leisure, Repose
Habit	Tradition, Practice, Addiction, Custom, Accustomed, Manner

www.ingramcontent.com/pod-product-compliance
Lightning Source LLC
Chambersburg PA
CBHW041510120626
46551CB00018B/2372